PRAISE FOR ... *AND THE CHURCH ACTUALLY CHANGED*

"Using a dialogical format, Standish invites the reader into engaging conversations. This is 'conversational intelligence' at its best, wrapped in wisdom and relevancy."
— Peter L. Steinke, church consultant, author of *UPROAR: Calm Leadership in Anxious Times*

"This book touched on every state of my ministry in the past twenty years. Readable, relatable, and oh-so relevant—a *must*-read for clergy."
— Kym Lucas, Bishop, The Episcopal Church of Colorado

"Wow! *And the Church Actually Changed* may be the most practical, insight-packed, easy-to-read, realistic, and hope-inspiring church leadership book ever written. Graham Standish is the ideal person to write this book; he combines the experience of a pastor with the sensitivity of a counselor and the insight of a widely-read scholar. Enthusiastically recommended!"
— Brian D. McLaren, author/speaker/activist

"Graham Standish offers pastors hope that they can lead change, humor that chides us out of our sullen stubbornness, and wisdom for navigating some of the most difficult terrain of pastoral leadership. Like the expert coach that he is, Standish asks questions, observes behaviors that others miss, and offers an occasional kick in the pants to get us going. This is a fun and insightful book that will inspire as it instructs."
— Tod Bolsinger, Vice President and Chief of Leadership Forma-

tion, Fuller Seminary and author of *Canoeing the Mountains: Christian Leadership in Uncharted Territory*

"Rev. Dr. Standish offers us rare glimpses into the pivotal conversations that transform pastoral leadership. These discussions reside at the intersection of coaching, spiritual direction, consulting, and mentoring. They are thought-provoking invitations offering vocational insight and practical take-aways for those who wrestle with the privilege and challenge of parish ministry."
— Rev. Melissa L. Stoller, Director for Evangelical Mission and Assistant to the Bishop of the Southwestern Pennsylvania Synod of the ELCA

"Standish writes with the mind of a seasoned leadership coach, the heart of a pastoral counselor, and the soul of a spiritual sage. This gem of a guidebook offers hope and direction for pastors frustrated by stagnation and decline in their congregations. Practical and concrete teaching, rich illustrations, and hands-on exercises will shepherd leaders taking on change resistance."
— Susan Beaumont, consultant and author of *How to Lead When You Don't Know Where You're Going*

... And the Church Actually Changed

...AND THE CHURCH ACTUALLY CHANGED

Uncommon Wisdom for Pastors in an Age of Doubt, Division, and Decline

N. Graham Standish

FORTRESS PRESS

Minneapolis

... AND THE CHURCH ACTUALLY CHANGED

Uncommon Wisdom for Pastors in an Age of Doubt, Division, and Decline

Cover illustration: Michael Austin c/o Theispot
Cover design: Laurie Ingram

Print ISBN: 978-1-5064-6194-6
eBook ISBN: 978-1-5064-6195-3

To my great friends, Ralph Lowe and Connie Frierson, who have often been the sounding board for the million ideas swirling in my head.

Contents

INTRODUCTION

I've been a successful pastor.

To me, that sounds like a cocky, arrogant statement. Why? Why is it so hard to admit publicly that we've been successful pastors? In any other field, it might be okay to talk about our overall success, but not in ministry—or at least in mainline Protestant church ministry.

I certainly haven't had the kind of success that notable evangelical pastors have had. The church I led for twenty-two years never had the proverbial "from five members to 5,000 in five years" kind of growth. Not even close. Still, we did turn around a church that had been in decline for over twenty years. We almost tripled our membership, doubled our attendance, creatively expanded our mission and ministry, expanded our property, and renovated and expanded our building. Over the years, several researchers and writers studied us because of our unique approach to ministry, mission, and congregational life—an approach emphasizing spirituality, prayer, and discernment.

There's a reason it feels as though we're supposed to hide our success as pastors. By my unscientific estimation, 80 percent of all mainline Protestant churches are in decline. With so many churches declining, struggling pastors and members don't necessarily know what to think about churches that are doing well. And they don't spend time exploring what those churches are doing well, perhaps because they're afraid it may point out what they're not doing well. It reminds me of what a woman said to me after we started hosting a parenting class at her request, but then she never showed up: "I was worried that they'd tell me I was a bad parent."

I think if most pastors talked with the pastors of churches that are doing well, they'd learn a lot about what they could do well, but they

1

would have to get over the fear they might be outed for being "bad." The truth is that pastors of healthy, successful churches like to mentor others to create healthy churches.

I've often wondered what's allowed me to be successful in ministry. Haven't all of us pastors had the same basic seminary training? Aren't we all coming from the same perspective? This is where I realize I'm different.

I don't have any particular charismatic skill that sets me apart from other pastors. I don't have any special pastoral powers. I wasn't trained in any special program grooming pastors for success. My field placement was in a rapidly declining church. As a seminary student, I don't know that I distinguished myself as a rising talent.

I did have one specific talent, though. I am acutely aware of what I don't know, and I'm tenaciously willing to get training for it, even—or especially—if it comes from sources other pastors shun. I know what I don't know, and I'm willing to learn from those who do know. And I don't care from whom I learn it as long as they are people who've proven they know. I'm also willing to eschew traditional training if it's clear this training historically hasn't worked.

Periodically, I've been asked whether my seminary training has helped me in my ministry. As I've reflected on this, I've come to realize maybe only 20 percent of my skill comes from seminary, 20 percent from my training as a therapist, 30 percent from my training in spiritual formation, and 30 percent from a whole slew of other fields and disciplines that are part of neither most pastors' typical training nor their fields of interest. I've been willing to learn from trainers, writers, and thinkers whom many in the mainline Protestant church either don't know or have discounted because they belong to the wrong Christian sect, have the wrong theology, or aren't theological enough.

Too many mainline Protestant pastors have narrow fields of study and interest. The anthropologist-turned-business journalist Gillian Tett coined a term describing this narrowness: *the silo effect:*

People often live in separate mental and social "ghettos," talking and coexisting only with people like us. In many countries, politics is polarized. Professions seem increasingly specialized, partly because technology keeps becoming more complex and sophisticated, and is only understood by a tiny pool of experts.[1]

She's describing what plagues much of mainline Protestant church ministry. We pastors tend to read and study theology, scholarly biblical writings, and works that reflect only our strongly held ideological perspectives. We don't study and read outside of our comfort zones. If we're progressive, we don't read insights coming from evangelicals, and vice versa. We might read a theological or even practical book on church leadership, but we won't read books on secular organizational theory and leadership. We don't dip into the incredible insights coming from the fields of organizational psychology, motivational theory, family systems theory, narrative therapy, cognitive behavioral therapy, neuroscience, sociology, anthropology, game theory, and so much more. We've created a mainline Protestant silo that keeps us from dialoguing with so many people and so many fields that could help us turn around our decline.

A pastor reminded me of this recently when he said, "We have to take mission proposals to our board so the board can decide if it's appropriate."

"Why?" I asked.

"Because that's what the Presbyterian Book of Order says we're supposed to do."

"But your Book of Order has basically been teaching us a model for ministry that inhibits zeal for mission. Why do we need to follow what it says?"

"I don't know," he said. "It's what I've been trained to do."

I learned nondenominational churches don't follow the typical Book of Order path. If someone has a passion for mission, leaders give permission for them to pursue it and help find funding for it. They nurture the mission while the proverbial fire is hot. They don't force it through a process that could take several months and lead to diminishing zeal. But this pastor, like so many other mainline Protestant clergy, never read works from nondenominational sources because they don't fit in the mainline Protestant silo.

My strength has been a willingness to step out of my Presbyterian silo and to browse all sorts of other silos. I constantly read and study outside of my comfort zone, which is actually how I ended up becoming a pastor. I didn't originally go to seminary to become a pastor. I went because I was a therapist and had a passion for addressing spiritual issues that arose in counseling sessions during a time when psychology looked skeptically and sometimes disapprovingly at religion and spirituality. Thus, I entered a dual program between Pittsburgh Theological Seminary and the University of Pittsburgh so I could get both a Master of Divinity and a Master of Social Work by studying counseling and the spiritual, not realizing how much more theological than spiritual seminary would be.

While I was studying for both degrees, I felt called to become an associate pastor, which came as a surprise to me. It was not how I had envisioned my life, and I followed the call grudgingly. As an associate pastor, I still felt inadequate to address the spiritual hunger I felt within our church and throughout our culture, especially from those calling themselves "spiritual but not religious." So, I began a course of self-study, regularly going to a bookstore that specialized in books on spirituality and devouring each one I could find.

My passion for learning more about Christian spirituality eventually led me to get a PhD in formative spirituality from Duquesne University. I thought this might be an avenue to teach in the area of spirituality; but once again, I was surprised I felt called to pastor a church and to help create a church rooted in a deeper spiritual approach that could be considered spiritual *and* religious. I finally felt like I knew how to create a church with a deeper spirituality, as well as address spiritual issues that arose in counseling.

Unfortunately, I became aware I had never really been trained in leadership, especially transformational leadership. I knew how to be the pastor of an established church, but not how to pragmatically transform an established church into one more deeply spiritual in a way that didn't lead to crippling conflict. So I began working on my transformation as a leader.

I began applying principles from my training as a therapist, such as overcoming resistance, understanding triangulation, modifying behavior, and much more. I also started taking nearly every leadership training program the now-defunct Alban Institute offered. Furthermore, I began attending nondenominational church training events. I often felt like an outlier because I was a denominational pastor who didn't speak their language or share their backgrounds.

I also embarked on a self-study in leadership. I read many books on church transformation by evangelical and semi-evangelical writers, such as Rick Warren, Erwin McManus, Robert Webber, Leonard Sweet, Henry Blackaby, John Maxwell, and Brian McLaren. They knew what they were doing as leaders and I didn't, so I needed to learn from them.

Still, I felt something was missing in their writings too. They were always writing to a theologically narrow audience and had to be careful about how they articulated their insights. This led me to begin an intensive self-study in secular organizational leadership, inhaling books on how to create harmonious organizations, how companies become great, how companies fail, how to motivate people, how to lead through transformation, how to integrate right- and left-brain thinking in leadership, and so much more. I read writers, such as Jim Collins, Simon Sinek, Annie McKee and Richard Boyatzis, Daniel Pink, and Stephen Covey. I also studied marketing principles, principles of audio/visual presentations, website design, social media, etc. I visited many, many silos and all of them nourished me.

I haven't always enjoyed all of this study, but it's always helped me become a better pastor. I no longer let restrictive theological perspectives, vocational choices, or fear of my ignorance get in my way. I'm a moderately progressive, spiritually oriented Presbyterian, but I'm willing to learn from a variety of thinkers regardless of their orientation or perspectives.

Through all of this training, my passion has become helping other pastors create healthier churches by leading them out of their silos. I started along this path as a spiritual director back in the mid-1990s. I slipped into clergy coaching in the early 2000s, before I even knew there was such a thing, in response to my gradual realization that these pastors' spiritual struggles were rooted in leadership struggles.

They were experiencing conflict as they tried to change their churches (it's easy to feel abandoned by God when it feels as though everyone is criticizing us). But the problem wasn't their being abandoned by God. It was their failure to lead transition in a way that motivated and bonded people as a community. Their prayer habits could always be improved; but more importantly, they had developed bad leadership habits that needed adjusting.

Getting pastors to open up to other possibilities can be difficult. We have such resistance to ideas, concepts, and practices outside of our comfort zones. I remember working with a very conservative, evangelical pastor years ago as we talked about his changing perspective on his relationship with God. His growing spiritual awareness reminded me of what Marcus Borg had written in his book *The Heart of Christianity*. So I suggested he read the book and lent him my copy. He returned it a month later and I asked him how it went.

"I loved it," he replied. "It really spoke to me. But the whole time I read it, my hands were shaking because I felt so guilty, like I was committing sin by reading Borg. He's been so criticized by so many pastors in my circle who consider him bad and wrong and liberal and perhaps evil. The shaking got so bad, I couldn't read it anymore, so I got only halfway through."

If we're going to revitalize our churches, we need to step out of our silos and integrate a variety of perspectives into our leadership. This book is an attempt to help. I'm sharing some of what I've learned from these atypical, often non-church sources, as well as from my years of experience as a spiritual director and clergy coach. It's aimed to help not only pastors specifically, but church leaders in general, to gain new insight into their leadership by tapping into insights from the fields of counseling, organizational theory, motivational theory, narrative theory and therapy, spirituality, business dynamics, systems theory, and much more. This book encourages pastors to step out of their cocoons of like-minded thinkers.

This book also shares these thoughts through the context of my present vocation as the executive director of a faith-based counseling agency and the director of our Caring for Clergy and Congregations program. I currently work with about twenty-eight pastors one-on-one, both locally and by teleconference across the United States, Canada, and Australia. I also consult with churches and run groups for pastors. Many of the issues I address in this book are ones that consistently arise throughout my work with pastors.

Each chapter in this book is written as if it were a one-on-one clergy coaching session with a pastor struggling over a specific issue in their church. None of these chapters is a verbatim transcript of any session with any one pastor. Instead, each chapter reflects and addresses real issues brought up in individual sessions, groups, consultations, or informal conversations with other pastors. When the chapters reflect actual discussions in sessions, I've changed the circumstances, so no one reading this book can identify any pastor from the descriptions or conversations. What you should know about all of them, though, is all of these pastors share one incredible trait: they've all stepped out of their silos and sought ways to become better leaders. They've all been willing to do the hard and often painful work of developing self-awareness and learning new ways of being pastors. I'm so grateful to have been able to learn from them as they've stretched me.

Finally, I want to express my deep gratitude to so many people who have influenced this book. Specifically, I want to thank the Revs. J. J. Lynn, Tara Lynn, C. F. Hoffman, Jennifer Fuhr, Melissa Stoller, Sarah Robbins, Sean Myers, Cameron Freese, Tim Archibald, Becky Branch-Trevathan, Nick Marlatt, Kevin Long, Meta and Stephen Cramer, Tom Harmon, Cinda Isler, Emily Miller, Don Coleman, Nathan Loudon, Kris Schondelmeyer, Jae Cho, Beth Wierman, Diane Flynn, Susan Rothenberg, Allyn Itterly, Brian Evans, Jennifer McCurry, David Hanssen, Brian Swann, Doug Marshall, John Corbett, Bob Cheyney, Ray Medina, Dena Roy, Jeff Hochstetler, Sheldon Sorge, Tammy Wiens, and so many, many more. Also, I want to give special thanks to both Richard and Diana Bass, who gave me many opportunities to flesh out and write about my insights through previous books.

Thank you to the members of Calvin Presbyterian Church in Zelienople, Pennsylvania, and Trinity Presbyterian Church in Butler, Pennsylvania. Both congregations have had an amazing influence on my life. I especially want to thank my colleagues at Calvin Church—Bruce Smith, Toni Schlemmer, DeWayne Segafredo, Dahn Kilroy, and Michelle Sheper—who were so instrumental in making Calvin Church a wonderfully thriving church.

Additionally, I'm so thankful for the leadership staff, therapists, and board members of Samaritan Counseling, Guidance, and Consulting, especially Susan Young, Luci Ramsey, and Beth Healey. This has been an incredible place that keeps me growing, as well as allows me to engage my passions and calling as a spiritual director, coach, group leader, and consultant with pastors and churches. Working in a place where I can integrate so many different ways of thinking is amazing.

I cannot say how much I've appreciated the opportunity to work again with my amazing editor, Beth Gaede, who was the incredible editor of three of my previous books for Alban Books and was open to this idea in her present position with Fortress Press. Rarely do we get the opportunity to work with people who consistently make us better in our craft; but under her tutelage, I feel like I finally know how to write.

Finally, I want to share my deep appreciation for two people who have been incredibly influential to me: the Rev. Connie Frierson and the Rev. Ralph Lowe—two of my best friends and people who have incredible insights and have also engaged in thinking outside the box with me.

Oh, and what does the title mean? It's a phrase several pastors I've worked with have said over the years: "I've been doing what we've talked about, *and the church actually changed!*"

NOTE

1. Gillian Tett, *The Silo Effect: The Peril of Expertise and the Promise of Breaking Down Barriers* (New York: Simon & Schuster Paperbacks, 2015), 13.

1

ARE WE LEADING FROM A FOUNDATION?

Len is a Lutheran pastor of a relatively wealthy suburban church in Maryland. We meet once a month by video teleconference. He has been in his present church for about five years, arriving there after a somewhat successful ministry in a smaller church north of Baltimore. He was asked by the bishop to help this church reverse its long-term stagnation.

Before his arrival, the church had been in moderate decline for over fifteen years. Some younger families have joined the church since Len's start, but the deaths of many of its older members have been the main driver of the decline. Since his installation, he has officiated thirty-five to forty funerals. Members have not been leaving the church for another, although periodically a family would leave for a nondenominational, contemporary church. The feedback he's received from members is that most of the church's members like a more traditional, liturgical style of worship, although not exclusively. They are open to newer styles but not wholesale changes. He complains that the church seems to lack passion for anything.

Len sought spiritual direction/clergy coaching as a way to help him improve his well-being and to find different ways of leading the church. He felt his growing frustration was beginning to hamper his leadership. We had met for five sessions over six months before this meeting.

****

9

Graham: How're you doing this afternoon?

Len: Eh! I could be better, . . . I could be worse.

Graham: That's gloomy. You kind of look tired. Tell me what's going on.

Len: Eh, . . . I'm just tired of the apathy in my church. We've talked about this before. It just seems like no matter what ideas I have, they're like, "Okay, pastor. Whatever you want." Then they don't follow up.

Graham: Yeah, and you wish they'd be more passionate. You wish they'd have some of the passion the members had when you were in your last church. I imagine you feel a bit beat down, . . . defeated.

Len: Beat down, maybe, . . . not defeated quite yet, but I could be moving in that direction. Yes, I wish they'd be more passionate. I'll have been there for five years two months from now. I expected a lot more from them. I know before I came, the bishop had said they were struggling to do anything, but so was my last church, and we managed to increase our mission and ministry some. Here, it's so sluggish.

I've really tried everything I know to do, but they don't respond. Last week may have been my lowest point. We had our council meeting, and I got really angry with them. I started shouting at them for not doing more. It was like my anger had become some sort of darkness that possessed me for a while. I was just looking at myself yell like I was watching a movie. It was me yelling, but it wasn't me, if you know what I mean. I didn't know how to stop. Then, when I was done, I didn't know what to do. I just sat there breathing hard. They stared at me. I then tried to move us on, but the rest of the meeting was just weird.

Graham: Do you get angry at your board a lot?

Len: Not outwardly, but inwardly, yeah. I think I'm angry at them all the time.

Graham: Because they're not doing more?

Len: Yeah. Do you think it's okay to get angry at your council at your church?

Graham: Do you?

Len: I used to believe it was, mainly because when I was in seminary, they often talked about righteous anger like Jesus had. You know, turning over tables, calling the Pharisees and Sadducees viper broods, and stuff like that. I think I'm changing my mind, though. Jesus got killed for yelling at people. But what do you think? Can you be righteously angry at your board?

Graham: Righteously angry? I guess part of the answer is whether anything we do in a church rises to the level of Jesus's anger. But let's put that aside for the moment. When I was pastor at my previous church, I developed a rule: you can get angry at the session—uh, board (that's what Presbyterians call our board)—exactly one time, and you better find a way to heal it pretty quickly. Or you better find a way to short-circuit it as you're yelling.

I had a situation years ago when I got really angry with our board, and it was the only time they ever saw me that way. It was very early in my ministry there, and some of our board members accused me of wanting to get rid of our drama ministry. We had a pretty big drama ministry that involved a lot of our members and people from the community. What they accused me of wasn't true. I valued the drama ministry and secretly contributed money to it to keep it afloat. The problem was the ministry used the sanctuary for its plays, meaning there were Sundays where I led worship in front of a *Godspell* or *Jesus Christ Superstar* set. I was okay with it, but not if it completely disregarded how we looked on Sunday morning for worship.

Anyway, there was one Sunday where they didn't complete the set. As I looked at the front, there were colored cloths slung haphazardly across the unfinished set and tools lying on the chancel floor. It was a mess. I was pretty upset and forced the music director to stop preparing for worship and help me get the front presentable for worship. He wasn't happy with me, but he did it.

A few weeks after the last play was over, I created a task force to set some boundaries on the drama ministry. It was a task force of both cast members from the play and those who had constantly come up to me asking that, in the future, we get the plays out of the sanctuary and into our fellowship hall. The rumor started that the task force was intended to get rid of the plays.

So, at our board meeting, I was accused of plotting to get rid of the drama ministry, which wasn't true. I got really upset, as you would imagine anyone would in that situation. We were in a discussion about the task force and its proposal when an elder said, "Graham, I had one of the members say to me, 'Graham has wanted to get rid of our plays ever since he came here.'" My anger started burning slowly, and soon I was over-the-top angry. Like you said, I was in a rage, and I saw my anger almost like an observer as it took control of me. Then I realized I was angry and knew I was about to lose the whole board if I continued, but I didn't know how to get out of it. In a moment of inspiration, I suddenly knew I had to turn my anger into something playful.

In a twinkling of inspiration, maybe from God, I remembered a *Saturday Night Live* skit with John Belushi doing a recurring character who would give an op-ed piece during the "Weekend Update" section. He'd start out talking about an issue and would slowly get worked up about it. He would become angrier and angrier and angrier until he was in a full-blown rage. And he would eventually say something like, "They could have given me back my money, but *noooooooo!*" Then he would clutch his heart and fall over in his chair. Then they'd continue with the "Weekend Update."

The inspiration was that I was in a John-Belushi moment. So, I started turning my anger into something silly, and I said, "All I hear is I'm against this, I'm against that. I try to help them see I'm not, but *noooooooo!*" And then I clutched my chest and fell over backward in my chair. Clearly they thought I was imitating John Belushi, and it caught them by surprise. I slowly got up and said, "Okay, anger time's over. I had my John Belushi moment. Let me try to respond in a normal way." They were laughing at me, but not really sure what was real and what was not. I eventually apologized for getting defensive and told them I would do better in the future. I salvaged it.

The problem is sometimes when pastors get angry at boards, they never salvage it.

Len: Yeah, I don't think I salvaged it. I wish I would have thought about the John Belushi thing, but I'm a bit young for that. I didn't start watching till the Dana Carvey years. But I get your point. Don't get angry.

Graham: Not quite "don't get angry," but don't let your anger possess you. Don't let it rip apart your relationship with your board, because that's the most important relationship in the church. If you're against them, then they begin resisting everything.

Len: So, what do I do?

Graham: You mean now that you've been angry, or whenever you get angry?

Len: I guess both.

Graham: I think it starts with being self-aware of your anger and how it starts to control you. Let's explore this a bit. Do you show your anger a lot?

Len: Not really. That was an exception. I don't think my other ways of dealing with it are much better. When I get angry—

Graham: Let me stop you for a moment. Let's not just start with anger. My sense is you get frustrated way before you get angry, so let's start there. What do you do when you start getting frustrated?

Len: I think I tend to get snarky or sarcastic.

Graham: And when you do that, what are you trying to do?

Len: What do you mean?

Graham: Snark and sarcasm are strategies to try to get them to do something. What is it you're trying to get them to do?

Len: I don't know . . . maybe trying to shame them into doing what I want, but it's a bit more passive-aggressive.

Graham: And when that doesn't work, it can spill over into anger that just becomes aggressive and maybe even rage?

Len: Yeah.

Graham: So, what are you trying to accomplish?

Len: I think I'm using shame as a weapon to try to get them to do what I want.

Graham: Stop here for a moment and see if you hear yourself. It's what *you* want them to do. Not what God wants, not what might be best, but what *you* want. Can you hear that?

Len: Yeah, but I don't really like hearing it. Thanks!

Graham: Listen, I know. We invest a helluva lot of time in our visions and plans. It's hard when they don't get it, and even harder when they don't share our passions. I think ministry is one of *the* most frustrating vocations possible. Most of the people you're work-ing with are volunteers, so you can't use increased or decreased pay as an incentive nor firing as a corrective. It's why I emphasize so much the importance of our relationships with them. Anyway, it's still hard when they don't get or share the passion for what we're try-ing to do.

Len: Yep! I think I'm always trying to get them to do what I want, now that I think about it. I don't know how much I've ever asked them, or even asked myself, to do what God wants. I just sort of fol-low whatever program's gotten my passion. It's funny . . . I've heard you talk a lot about listening for what God wants us to do, and I agree with it, but that's not the same as saying I try to do it or I ever accomplish it. I guess I keep hoping if they do what I want to do, God will comply by agreeing with what I want to do. (chuckles) . . . Don't you think it would be nice if God would do what we want instead of the other way around?

Graham: Yes, but that would make God a genie instead of God. Let's hold off on the listening-to-God thing a bit and see if we can come back to it. I want to explore what you've been trying to do. We'll connect that with God's will later. What programs have you tried to get them to become passionate about?

Len: I've tried to get them to buy into the NCD, but it was like talking to cheese.

Graham: NCD? Cheese?

Len: Sorry, my father used to say talking to people who wouldn't listen was like talking to cheese. He'd say people are like cheese—soft and sometimes smelly. Anyway, I mean Natural Church Development.[1] It's a program based on the studies of thou-sands of growing churches in America and Europe done by a guy named Christian Schwartz. Our bishop wanted all of us to read a book about it several years ago, and I really liked it. It got me jazzed up to make real changes in the church.

Graham: That's such a funny thought—people are like cheese. I am aware of NCD—I just forgot. I read their book about fifteen years ago. Lots of good stuff in there, but I also wondered if their studies focus too much on nondenominational churches that are much less resistant to new approaches. NCD does a good job of talking about what needs to be done but not necessarily about how to get them implemented with highly resistant congregations. Anyway, what happened when you tried?

Len: I had our council read their book, and we discussed everything. Most of the council wouldn't read the chapters, and the ones who participated in the discussions talked mostly about why we couldn't do this or that.

Graham: Yikes! That's discouraging.

Len: Yeah . . . you can see why I got angry.

Graham: I can, but I also have a question: what do you think they heard was your implicit message when you suggested that book, and as they read it?

Len: What do you mean?

Graham: Well, there's a reason you wanted them to read the book and discuss it, right?

Len: Yeah, I wanted them to read something about how to grow our church.

Graham: I'm sure they got that message, but what was the more negative message they heard from you in that? I mean, the implicit message they might have heard as criticism of them?

Len: Oh, wow, I never thought about that. I just thought if I gave them that book to read, they'd get it and want to move in that direction.

Graham: Right, but their reaction to you suggests they didn't get that message. What message do you think they got, even if it wasn't what you wanted to say to them?

Len: God! I feel so stupid. Why didn't I think of what they might have thought I was saying?

Graham: Because you actually care about them and want them to do better. It's like with kids. When we raise our voices with them, we're trying to help them to do better and have better lives. But that's not always what they hear. Kids can hear things we're not saying because criticism stings. What do you think your council might have heard?

Len: That they suck! That they're no good. That they've been

15

in decline for the past fifteen years because they're bad. And here I am coming in and telling them what they should have done all that time and they now have to change everything about themselves to become good. Graham, this is significant. I always just assumed whatever I suggest, they'll hear it as something good. It never occurred to me they'd hear something negative.

Graham: Well, this gets back to the frustration and anger. It seems like you get frustrated and angry with them for not meeting your expectations, and perhaps they resist you because you're not meeting theirs.

Len: Uh, I followed you on the first part, but what do you mean I'm not meeting theirs? They said they wanted to grow. I'm trying to help them do that. That was their expectation.

Graham: That's what they put on paper. And that was a paper created by some search committee or council. What do you think their real expectations were?

Len: I'm not sure I'm liking where we're going with this.

Graham: I'm sorry. I know. And I'm now worried you may be feeling about me the way you're worried they're feeling about you. You know, I'm supposed to push you deeper, but that doesn't mean it feels good for either you or me. I sort of have the same hopes for our work you hope for them—with what we're doing, you'll find a way to be more effective at leading them toward your vision. I'm sorry.

Len: It's okay. It's why I'm here. You're supposed to push me, and I'm supposed to not always like it. Okay, so, what were their *real* expectations? That's a good question. Clearly, it wasn't to grow like they said.

Graham: It may be still they wanted to grow. But it also may be they wanted to grow at a different pace, or they envisioned a different kind of growth than you did. Maybe they wanted the change to be slower. Or maybe they were hoping the change meant keeping more of the stuff they've loved—you know, bring in more people who are just like they already are and who will love the organ, or stuff like that. Let's change the word from *real*. What do you think their *deeper* expectations were?

Len: Uhhhhh . . . (slumps down in his chair) I think they wanted someone to come in and tell them they're good and loved and cared about, and God thinks they're good and loved and cared about. Maybe that was the change they wanted, because I don't think their previous pastor did that. And I don't think I've done that very much, either, which is funny, because that's who I wanted to be for them—a person they felt loved them. I've gotten frustrated and angry, and it's made me cranky.

Graham: Let me give you a bit of a pass on that, because you're not alone. I want to come back to how to be who and what you want to be, but I want to talk a bit about your expectations. The pass is you're a product of your training. You've been trained to try to get them to grow. You've been trained in seminary by reading theologies and ecclesiologies of what ideal churches should be like. You've read books—maybe even some of mine—that tell you what successful churches are doing. NCD is a good example, which doesn't mean their research or conclusions have been wrong or bad. But they do cause you to develop high expectations that may be unrealistic where you are. You've looked around at all the growing non-denominational churches and seen what they've done, showing you what may be possible. And you've been immersed in all the trends about what a healthy pastor is and does.

You've learned you're supposed to be the theologian-in-residence; you're supposed to create all sorts of discipleship groups to make them all disciples; you need to be missional and to get your church active in providing mission to the community; you're supposed to be a spiritual leader guiding them to a deeper spirituality; and you're supposed to be an authentically pastoral person who visits everyone at the drop of a hat. You've been taught by your seminary professors what really matters is the theological depth of your preaching. At the same time, you've seen enough of Joel Osteen to worry you have to be a dynamic and maybe slightly shallow preacher who attracts people to your church because of your charisma, which you may or may not have. And above all, you're the pastor of a struggling church that's been that way for a long time, and you're supposed to skillfully reverse their fortunes. You've been trained to have high expectations for them and yourself. The pass is these are all burdens others have put on you through your training. But is it really what you're called to do and be as a pastor? Is it really why God called you to that church? Is it really why the bishop asked you to go there?

Len: Don't forget I'm supposed to be a prophetic preacher, calling Israel back to God.

Graham: Oh yeah, and what they forgot to tell you was all those prophets got ignored, mocked, criticized, beaten, and sometimes killed. No wonder they spent so much time in the desert. "In the desert, you can remember your name, 'cause there ain't no one for to give you no pain."[2]

Len: America. "A Horse with No Name." I love it! Yeah, and I feel a bit like I've been in a desert.

Graham: Funny thing is even though we're told we're supposed to be prophetic in our preaching, I don't think that was the model of the apostles in Acts. They seemed to have a much more compassionate and positive preaching style. The few who were prophetic, like Stephen, got stoned to death.

What stands out to me is Paul's message in 1 Corinthians 9, where he says that to the Jews he became a Jew, to the Gentiles he became a Gentile, to the weak he became weak, so he could win them. He said he became all things to all people so he might save some—not all, but some. It makes me wonder if Paul had a different preaching style tailored to each one. He came out of the prophetic tradition, but in the move from Saul to Paul, did he then change his style from prophet to something else? Anyway, we're going down a bunny trail. My point was you have high expectations of them, and they have high expectations of you. What if your expectations of each other aren't meeting?

Len: Clearly, they aren't.

Graham: So, what if you changed tactics? What if you stopped focusing on your expectations for them, and perhaps even their expectations of you, and started leading out of something a bit deeper.

Len: Okay, I'm game. But first . . . I have no idea what you're talking about.

18

Graham: Yeah, it would be good if I'd explain what I mean first.

Len: It's okay, I kind of like these surprises. I'm getting used to them.

Graham: What I mean is this: what if you stopped trying to get them to meet your expectations and instead led them out of your principles? That's not the same as saying get rid of your vision for the church. But instead of focusing so much on how to get them to do what you want to reach *your* goals, what if you led out of a set of principles that built up trust, that would then build relationships, which would make attaining your vision easier?

Len: That sounds great. What do you mean by "leading out of my principles"?

Graham: I mean what are your leadership principles, those ways of interacting with parishioners you try to hold onto no matter what the situation is? What are the core principles you won't violate, even when things are going terribly wrong and downhill? If everyone's resisting you, what are the core principles you won't violate to try to get them to do what you want?

Len: (long pause) I'm not sure I have those principles. When they're not doing what I'm asking them to do, I sort of resort to anything that will get them to do it. So, there are times when I get critical or snarky or even aggressive. I don't think I have principles like the ones you're talking about.

Graham: Sure you do, but you may have forgotten them or not realized they're there or pushed them aside in your zeal to accomplish your vision.

Len: Yeah, I'm not sure I do have them.

Graham: Well, what's the foundation of your leadership?

Len: I think it's whatever new program or approach I'm trying. I think I try to imagine I'm the person who's written the book I've just read or whose workshop I've taken, and then I think I try to imitate how I imagine they might have acted. Maybe that's why I get so dissatisfied. I'm not them.

Graham: Maybe. So, what do you think your foundational principles are?

Len: I don't know. You keep asking me that. How do I find them?

Graham: Ummmm . . . that's a good question. Give me a second to think about that. I know I have strong leadership principles, but I'm not sure how I got them. Do you mind sitting there for a minute while I think? I realize that's kind of boring.

Len: No problem. I like seeing you stumped, so I'll just enjoy your being stumped.

Graham: Glad to be the in-flight entertainment. Give me a second . . . (long pause) I think I know how to find out. I realize I developed my principles out of the example set by a combination of people I've known personally and respected, as well as a number of really great figures and writers who've influenced me by both what they've taught and how they've lived.

Here are the ones I can think of. My father was a big influence because he was a federal judge who managed to treat everyone with respect, no matter who they were. When we were kids, there were times when we would go to restaurants or a gas station and have to wait because he was having a casual conversation with the server or attendant. He remembered little tidbits about their lives from previous times he was there, and he would always ask them about these things. They loved him because he genuinely cared about them. He had a prestigious position and a humble spirit.

I've also been influenced by Adrian van Kaam, whom I studied with at Duquesne University for my PhD in spiritual formation. He was a deeply humble man and yet perhaps the most brilliant person I've ever been around. And I learned so much from him about how to be deeply spiritual, humble, and normal at the same time.

I've also been influenced heavily by both Mahatma Gandhi and Martin Luther King Jr. They've been my religious heroes for their ability to take Jesus's teachings and draw on them in crisis situations. I've read many biographies and writings of both, and their constant focus on leading out of compassion while still being willing to take a stand for God's way is really influential for me.

Len: Gandhi was a Hindu, not a Christian. He wouldn't have read Jesus's teachings.

Graham: He was Hindu, but he studied the Gospels a lot and considered the Sermon on the Mount to be the greatest religious teaching of all time. He learned about it from reading Tolstoy. That's where he really got the idea of civil resistance.

Anyway, there are also many spiritual writers who've influenced me, and they all come from different traditions. I've been influenced by a Quaker named Thomas Kelly, who wrote my favorite book, *A Testament of Devotion*.[3] And a Presbyterian, Catherine Marshall, who wrote Presbyterian/Pentecostal-type books about God being involved deeply in our lives in response to prayer. Also, a Russian Orthodox priest named Father Arseny, who spent twenty-seven years in a Siberian gulag. He was amazing because instead of being constantly depressed, he decided he simply was where God called him to be, and his task was to serve in the gulag with love and compassion. And in the process, he transformed many, many lives. I also admire Elder Thaddeus of Vitovnica, a Russian Orthodox monk in Yugoslavia, who wrote about how our ways of thinking influence our awareness of God. Another is Corrie ten Boom, who held onto her faith, hope, and love while hiding Jews from Nazis. She was sent to a concentration camp, yet she never lost her desire to serve God even while there. Also, Brother Lawrence of the Resurrection, a seventeenth-century monk, and Frank Laubach, a twentieth-century missionary to the Philippines, who both wrote about carrying on a constant conversation with God and living in an intensive, immediate awareness of God at all times. Finally, both St. Patrick and St. Francis, who lived lives of deep service to God and others and who tried to be conduits between the eternal and this world.

All of them have influenced me. As I think about them, I can trace my principles. Realize these are off the top of my head, but I think about these principles a lot, and I'm aware of them especially when things aren't going the way I want them to go:

- Treat everyone with compassion and care, even if they're not treating me that way.
- Be both humble and normal at the same time, and look for ways to show understanding and care even while leading people outside of their comfort zones.
- Be willing to take a stand for what's right, but also make sure

I'm doing it in ways that treat others with respect and help them feel like they are being heard and respected.

- Always listen in and through others for what God may be saying, and be humble enough to hear through any situation whatever guidance God is giving me.
- Lead people to listen for what God wants, rather than leading them to what I want God to want.

Len: Wow! I don't know how much of that I have.

Graham: You have it. You just aren't as aware of it. So, let's just start with people you've admired and then move from there.

Len: I was thinking about that as you were talking. I know there are several people. I really admire Abraham Lincoln. I admired his ability not only to do what's right, but also to change his mind in doing what's right. I read a book about him by Doris Kearns Goodwin where she talked about how he assembled a cabinet of rivals, and I would like to be able to do that. Or at least, I'd like to be able to treat people in a way that those who disagree with me could also support me because they feel like I support them.

Another is John F. Kennedy. He was assassinated before I was born, but I've read about him. I love how he could lead people by being positive and by challenging people to focus on how they can help others instead of trying to get others to always help them. He was positive, but also other-focused. I think I'm other-focused, but I'm not always positive. In fact, I'm often not, which is not the way I used to be.

That leads me to my third one. I admire Phil Dunphy.

Graham: Wait. Phil Dunphy?

Len: Yeah, the guy married to Claire on the television show, *Modern Family.*

Graham: Okay (laughing), I know who he is. Why Phil Dunphy?

Len: Because he's always positive and never lets whatever happens get him down. He's always really sensitive and simultaneously looking to make people around him feel better. He gets criticized, but he never lets it get him down for too long. And he's creative. He's always trying new things. Sometimes they're really stupid, but he has fun. I haven't had fun in my ministry for a long time. I think I need to be more like Phil Dunphy.

Graham: Those are great! I love them! Okay, what I want you to do between now and our next time together is to do an exercise. I want you to make a list of those people you admire, leaving space after each name so you can write down the essential qualities you admire in them. Then I want you to turn that list into a separate list of leadership principles you want to hold onto and that will become your foundation for leading people to your vision. Make these your foundation, not your vision. You can still have the vision, but make these into principles you won't violate, no matter how bad things get. I'd even suggest you take an afternoon or morning off to sit somewhere calming and centering where you can reflect and put this together. And don't forget to ask God to guide you in this.

Len: I can do that. What if I spend Friday afternoon at my friend's church? They have a great room that looks out over their sanctuary. I can sit there.

Graham: Sounds great. Don't forget to take coffee with you.

Len: Oh, I never go anywhere without my coffee.

Graham: I know. Let's end here and pick all of this up next time.

FOLLOW-UP EMAIL FROM LEN

pastorlen@fauxemail.net[4]

Subject: Admired Leader Exercise

Hi, Graham,

I know we aren't chatting again until November, but I thought if I got this done, I might get a gold star for enthusiasm.

I also thought it might give you time to ponder [this] before we next meet. I'm not sure if what I have is accurate about the people in question, but what I've got here is an identification of how I feel when I hear them or read about them. Hope it makes sense.

Len

The Reverend Leonard Cathartic

Senior Pastor

Trinity Lutheran Church

Leaders Who Resonate with Me

JFK

We choose to go to the moon. We choose to go to the moon in this decade and do the other things, *not because they are easy, but because they are hard*, because that goal will serve to organize and measure the best of our energies and skills, because that challenge is one that we are willing to accept, one we are unwilling to postpone, and one which we intend to win, and the others too.[5]

Principles: Optimistically and hopefully looking forward.

Joe Biden

To me, he seems like a man who, despite tragedy, operates with *hopefulness, integrity, dignity, and passion*. He seems to be a person who will work with people rather than against them for the sake of it. He seems like a man who sees people as important and that his vocation to his country is more important than any partisanship. I have seen him talk about the importance of hope and purpose.

He said in an interview, "Caring about your colleague as they're dealing with a sick parent, or their child has graduated from college, or the child just was in an accident. That's the stuff *that fosters real relationships, breeds trust, [and] allows you to get things done* in a complex world."[6]

Principles: Integrity, dignity, and passion. Building trusting relationships.

Former US Navy Admiral and Navy SEAL William H. McRaven

I first saw this guy on a Facebook video and I found it so inspiring. What I took from this is a voice of *integrity* and *practical wisdom*. The words of his speech that grab me are:

To pass SEAL training, there are a series of long swims that must be completed. One is the night swim. Before the swim, the instructors joyfully brief the trainees on all the species of sharks that inhabit the waters off San Clemente. They assure you, however, that no student has ever been eaten by a shark—at least not recently. But you are also taught that if a shark begins to circle your position—stand your ground. Do not swim away. Do not act afraid. And if the shark, hungry for a midnight snack, darts towards you—then summon up all your strength and punch him in the snout, and he will turn and swim away. There are a lot of sharks in the world. If you hope to complete the swim, you will have to deal with them. So, if you want to change the world, don't back down from the sharks.

If I have learned anything in my time traveling the world, it is the power of hope. The power of one person—Washington, Lincoln, King, Mandela, and even a young girl from Pakistan, Malala—one person can change the world by giving people hope.

Start each day with a task completed. Find someone to help you through life. Respect everyone.

Know that life is not fair and that you will fail often. *But if you take some risks, step up when the times are toughest, face down the bullies, lift up the downtrodden, and never, ever give up—if you do these things, then the next generation and the generations that follow will live in a world far better than the one we have today.*

And what started here will indeed have changed the world—for the better.[7]

Principles: Capacity to take some risks to inspire with practical wisdom.

GEORGE VI

Most of this is based on my watching *The King's Speech*. I think what captures my feeling on this is expressed by Winston Churchill [while] giving some insight into King George's personality in the speech he made on the king's death, saying: "We thought of him when calmly, when without ambition or want of self-confidence, he assumed the heavy burden of the crown and succeeded his brother whom he loved and whom he had rendered perfect loyalty."

Another observation was George VI, instead of taking his perceived shortcomings and hiding them behind a shield of pomp and bluster, allowed this vulnerability to show. It also appears while he had a reluctance to lead, King George and his queen provided hope and inspiration for many during one of the most troubled times in Great Britain's history.

Principles: Lead with hope and inspiration and without an overriding ambition.

PHIL DUNPHY

Just for a bit of fun. In saying that, there is something about Phil Dunphy I really relate to. I think it is in his words, he is "original, imaginative, fearless."

Principles: Leadership that is original, imaginative, fearless.

The leadership principles that came from a retiring lieutenant colonel I heard recently at a military base really resonated with me:

1. Embrace mission command, delegate down, and empower your team.
2. Park your aspirations, and be frank and fearless in your approach.
3. Be kind to yourself, exercise, and endeavor to put your family first always.

Actually, the one that really resonates in the context of our conversation is point 2. I think there is something important in putting your aspirations aside to lead with integrity so you can be frank and fearless in your approach. I see too many people who lead with a sense of aspiring rather than inspiring (if you know what I mean). I want to be a leader who *inspires* and *motivates*.

26

So, looking at what my principles of leadership might be:

1. *Lead optimistically and hopefully, looking forward to the future.*
2. *Lead with integrity, dignity, and passion, seeking to build trusting relationships.*
3. *Lead with a capacity to take calculated risks to inspire and motivate with practical wisdom.*
4. *Lead with hope and inspiration, and without an overriding ambition.*
5. *Lead with originality, imagination, fearlessness.*

I've also toyed with shortening this to the acronym WWPDD? Or "What Would Phil Dunphy Do?"

Blessings,

Len

FURTHER THOUGHTS

We live in a time when many models for ministry compete with each other and confuse us. I've been around long enough to have been trained or influenced by most of them or have just been aware of them. I've also been around long enough to have failed in them, floundered with them, created hybrids out of them, or learned to ignore them.

For example, when I was in seminary, the dominant model was the *pastoral care model*. I remember reading a book in seminary that basically said the pastor's main task was visitation and good pastors will visit all members at least once or twice a year. I bought into the model completely. I had been a therapist and have a Master of Social Work. I loved the idea of visiting people and being able to deal with concerns before they became issues. My first position in ministry was as an associate pastor for pastoral care.

As I progressed in ministry, I realized this was a flawed model. First off, I grew tired of *just* visiting after a while. I liked it, but not all the time, every day. Plus, it became hard to focus on other tasks, such as creating programs, teaching classes, staffing or running committees, reading, and preaching. I soon realized I could choose to lead a church to grow, or I could maintain the church by visiting, but I couldn't do both. Each one required too much time and attention. I chose to focus on growing the church and trained others to visit.

The pastoral care model replaced the *pastor as preacher* model, which focused on the pastor as mainly the preacher and teacher. (My tradition, the Presbyterian Church [USA], has tried to re-emphasize this by changing our designation to "Teaching Elder" rather than the previous title, "Minister of Word and Sacrament.") His—and back then it was primarily "his"—role was to spend most of the week in *his* "study" (not office), studying the Bible and reading deep works of theology. Then it was *his* responsibility to provide an erudite, deep, and powerful sermon on Sunday that would change people's lives. The problem was it wasn't working; people complained they got nothing out of such lofty sermons. Hence, the move to the pastoral care model. The nondenominational world kept a focus on preaching but with an emphasis on simple, practical, accessible sermons.

The pastoral care model changed for me after I attended a seminar in 1991 called "Can the Pastor Do It Alone?" The presenters called into question the idea pastors are the ones primarily responsible for pastoral care. They taught that pastoral care was also the responsibility of the congregation, and if the pastor does it all, that practice then inhibits the building up of community by not calling on others in the community to be primary carers.

The pastoral care model was replaced by the *discipleship* model. It taught that churches needed to "make disciples of all nations" (Matt 28:19). The focus of this model was to create small discipleship groups. I loved this idea because I had been trained in and practiced group therapy, and I had been trained in spiritual direction to do a small group form of spiritual direction (what our teachers called "direction-in-common"). Over time, I created small spiritual discipleship groups that ran for many years and were quite successful.

When I became a solo pastor, I came face-to-face with the limitations of the discipleship movement. It was rooted in new, nondenominational, contemporary churches that started in often white, transient, suburban developments where people were mostly new to the area and didn't know anyone. The small discipleship groups were a great way of helping people make connections. The problem in established churches is often the church itself, or many of the committees and program groups (choir, knitting circle, the old guys who gathered for breakfast every Thursday), were already small groups. It's hard to start a small group program in a place that doesn't feel the need for more small groups.

Eventually, I was able to create hybrid small groups around people's interests and struggles. Instead of having a lot of small groups all studying similar resources, we created small groups around specific interests. We established men's and women's devotional groups based on the practice of spiritual reading—reading classic and enduring spiritual books from across traditions and eras.[8] These groups are still going eighteen and twenty years later, respectively, even as the members have changed. We created a small weekly prayer group, as well as two weekly contemplative prayer groups. We even created groups based on specific topics such as near-death experiences, the connection between science and faith, women's issues, financial health, and more.

I was very much a part of the *spiritual leadership* movement, as shown by three books I wrote that explored how to bring prayer, discernment, and spirituality into church life. As such, I developed ways of integrating prayer and discernment into decision-making, offered training in spiritual practices, and created prayer opportunities (prayer vigils, outdoor labyrinths, and retreats). In working with pastors on this as a spiritual director and coach, I realized as wonderful as this model can be, it's hard to gain traction for it in churches that are in survival mode because members worried about survival have a hard time with prayer and discernment.

I've also seen the rise of the *missional church* movement, which emphasizes getting people involved in mission rooted in the surrounding culture as the way to get churches growing again. Through my church experiences and my work with others, I've seen its limitations. Again, churches in survival mode have a hard time moving into meaningful ministry and mission because their focus is inward and self-protective, while mission requires a more mature "other-focus."

Our church was very missional, but that emphasis arose out of our spiritual focus. As people became more mature spiritually and discerned more intentionally and regularly, they heard the call to embody their faith and love in tangible action. We had a lot of missional activity, but it was because people were encouraged to listen and act, and our church was set up to support them in their calling. For example, we supported members in starting a monthly dance night for older single adults, an afterschool program for at-risk teens, a mission collecting old bicycles to refurbish and send to a Native American reservation, and a fund to help people in impoverished situations who were facing evictions, medical problems, and other crises.

The takeaway is that we can have a vision for many different approaches for ministry. The variety of models speaks to the variety of ways God calls churches to act and the recognition that all churches are part of one body and therefore may be called to unique ministries and missions.

The one constant in leadership isn't the vision; it's the principles we hold in leading people to whatever vision we articulate. The principles of our leadership are more important than our vision or program. If we lead in a way that is compassionate, respectful, collaborative, trusting, and faithful, we will be followed, even if we don't have much of a clearly articulated vision. If we have a strong vision but our leadership is denigrating, dismissive, or exclusionary, people will hold onto the vision but find ways to get rid of us as leaders.

So what principles do you have for leadership? The following exercise might help you identify them.

LEADERSHIP PRINCIPLES

A) Thinking openly, but not too deeply, make a list of four to seven leaders you've admired, whether because of your particular connection or historical awareness of them. It may be good to avoid identifying Jesus, as well as biblical figures, as one of those leaders, so you can identify those who may be more personally relatable.

1.

2.

3.

4.

5.

6.

7.

B) Reflect on each one. Following each one's name, list the leadership qualities and principles about them you admire.

C) Culling from the list of leadership principles, now create a relatively succinct list of those leadership principles you want your leadership to reflect.

D) Reflecting more tangibly on specific leadership challenges, think of leadership struggles you've had in the past few years and how you might have led differently if you had been rooted in these principles. Be concrete and specific. You can choose to write these down or simply reflect imaginatively.

NOTES

1. Christian Schwartz, *Natural Church Development: A Guide to Eight Essential Qualities of Healthy Churches*, 3rd ed. (Bloomington, MN: ChurchSmart Resources, 1997).

2. "A Horse with No Name," album, track 5 on America, *America*, Warner Bros., 1972.

3. Thomas R. Kelly, *A Testament of Devotion* (San Francisco: HarperSanFrancisco, 1992).

4. This is an actual email from a pastor who engaged in this exercise and developed a set of principles from it. It was reprinted with permission, although the name and context have been changed.

5. John F. Kennedy, "Address at Rice University on the Nation's Space Effort," September 12, 1962, Rice University, transcript and video, https://tinyurl.com/y4f9fnmt.

6. Ester Bloom, "Joe Biden explains how this one trait can make you both happy and successful," CNBC, May 23, 2017, https://tinyurl.com/y5obp36b.

7. William H. McRaven, "Adm. McRaven Urges Graduates to Find Courage to Change the World," May 17, 2014, University of Texas–Austin, transcript and video, https://tinyurl.com/y3utdqyf.

8. A free list of suggested books and a guide to creating groups around spiritual readings can be found under the "Resources" tab at www.ngraham-standish.org.

ARE WE IN HARMONY
WITH OUR DNA?

Beth is a Methodist pastor of a suburban church in Pennsylvania. We meet once a month. She's been serving her church for about four years and previously was an associate pastor in a large, multi-staff, suburban church ten miles away. She is following a pastor who had been at this church for over sixteen years, an unusually long time for a Methodist pastor to be in one church.

The church stayed relatively stable over that period and even had a surge of growth between thirteen and six years earlier, but then attendance and membership flattened. They're something of a multigenerational church, with more members above age fifty than below, but there are some younger families. The attendance of some of those younger families has become spotty as their older children's activities get in the way. Some are reportedly visiting the nondenominational, contemporary church a half mile away. Beth's church is mostly traditional in its style, and that seems to be an issue for both Beth and the church. They aren't sure what to do to change, and Beth is frustrated because she has a vision of a much more vibrant and active congregation, with the integration of some contemporary elements. The resistance she's facing is causing her to become more cynical.

She sought spiritual direction/clergy coaching as a way to overcome her growing cynicism and the church's growing stagnation. We had previously met for two sessions.

****

Graham: Glad you're here, Beth. How are things since we talked last time?

Beth: Yuck! My cynicism's back. We talked last time about ways to let it go, and I've been trying. You talked to me about being aware of the cynicism, how and when it rises up, and then praying and giving it to God. I've been doing that, and it's mostly helped. But over the past week, the cynicism's been stronger than my prayer. It feels like it's poisoning me. I had a really bad sleep last night as I thought about asking the bishop and my district superintendent (DS) to find me a new church. But they don't like moving pastors early. That makes me feel even more stuck and cynical.

Graham: I get it. Cynicism and pessimism are like demon viruses. Once they infect us, they can grow and spread. And sometimes you just feel powerless as they darken everything.

Beth: They do. Our family went out for ice cream on Sunday afternoon because I just needed something to be cheerful. And it was nice. Then I spent the evening bumming out because I ate ice cream and I'm trying to lose weight. That made me feel even more pessimistic. The demon virus was spreading.

Graham: Yikes! It's like the cheery thing you do ends up making things darker.

Beth: At least for a little while. I did talk myself out of my guilt by bedtime.

Graham: We talked about this last time, this sense of cynicism that darkens everything else, which then causes you to become cynical in your ministry. It's like the cynicism feeds the darkness and the darkness feeds the cynicism.

Beth: Yeah, and I go through these periods of . . . of . . . I can't think of the right word—melancholy? Despondency? Disgust?

Graham: It might be all of those together.

Beth: Feels that way.

Graham: So, let's go back to what we talked about last time, about your cynicism and the church. I have some thoughts that may be helpful. But before I offer my ideas, do me a favor. Summarize your struggle and see if it's any clearer.

Beth: Basically, it's that I've been at this church for over two years

34

and it should be growing, but it isn't. I keep thinking about my initial conversations with them and my DS. I had come from a church that grew while I was there as an associate pastor, and so I feel like I know how to do it. The church said they wanted to grow. They told the DS and the bishop they wanted to grow and recapture some of the growth they'd had from Don, the previous pastor. That's why I was sent there. But when it came down to doing the things needed in order to grow, they resisted. They won't really do anything more than what they've already been doing.

They're in a suburban area with lots of new homes, and some of the other churches near us are growing. What's really frustrating is that some of our younger families are complaining to me that they want the church to be growing even more, and I don't know what to say to them other than I'm trying. When they talk about this in meetings, the older members kind of shush them.

Graham: Has it all been failing, or have some things worked?

Beth: What do you mean?

Graham: Are there some things they are good at doing? Are there some strengths?

Beth: They're kind of good at gossiping. Is that a strength?

Graham: Ha! I guess it depends upon how good the gossip is! Actually, it's not necessarily a complete weakness. It can mean there are some good relationships in the church.

Beth: Okay, then, they do kind of get along with each other. It's just frustrating they don't do much beyond being a social club.

Graham: So, what do they do well that's not gossip? What do they do well that would be considered ministry and mission?

Beth: Let's see. They're good at offering food bank contributions. They're also good at doing church dinners. And if there's a mission project to raise money for, they're good at doing that. They're good at chatting with each other during coffee after church. They're good at doing chatty cliques in general, which bugs me quite a bit because I'm not a chatty person like that. They also do some work for Habitat for Humanity; they'll volunteer to put up a house or walls or stuff like that. But it's like pulling teeth to try to get them to do anything else.

Graham: So, they don't really do much of the stuff that suburban churches typically do, like a preschool, a MOPS program, or parenting groups or stuff like that?

Beth: Nope. I've talked about a parenting group, but they just look at me like I'm speaking Klingon. Actually, most of what I suggest just elicits stares.

Graham: Did your predecessor have the same frustrations? Do you know?

Beth: I don't know. I've talked to him, and it seems like he was kind of into the chattiness and stuff.

Graham: What was he like as a pastor with them, especially in ways that are different from you?

Beth: He's kind of a "huggy" guy. I've seen him with some of our older members. He's always kissing the older women on the cheek and stuff like that.

Graham: Do you mean in an inappropriate way?

Beth: No, not like that. He's just like one of those old-time pastors who are happy visiting people and "shmushing" with them?

Graham: "Shmushing"?

Beth: Yeah, you know, kind of being a schmoozer in a mushy way—shmushy.

Graham: Got it! So he's kind of like an old country pastor?

Beth: Yeah.

Graham: I think I'm getting a picture. Tell me how your church started.

Beth: What do you mean? It's an old church. It started the way old churches start.

Graham: Right, when did it start and why?

Beth: Oh Gawd! I don't know. It's an old church. I guess it started in the 1850s.

Graham: Do you know why it started? Have you seen any kind of history of the church?

Beth: I did. I looked at some stuff when I first got there, but I don't remember much. Does it really matter?

Graham: Yeah, I think it does. All churches started for a reason, except for those that didn't stick around. And if they didn't stick around, it's because they didn't really have a deep guiding purpose. Churches that last have a compelling reason for being. Others simply fade away. Eventually, all churches fade away because they lose that founding purpose. That's why none of the original churches in Acts are still there. Generally, churches that last longer than fifteen to twenty years have had a strong, compelling founding purpose. Do you mind if I give you an example?

Beth: Sure . . . I mean, no—go ahead.

Graham: When I came to Calvin Presbyterian Church, my previous church, I did a study of their history. I was fortunate because they had just had their 150th anniversary a year before I came, and as part of that, one of the members did a small history. I also spent time talking with some of the older members to learn what they knew about why Calvin Church was founded and what it had been like in their memory. What I read and heard really helped me understand Calvin Church's history—its DNA. I'm a counselor at heart, so I like hearing people's stories, and I like hearing churches' stories.

The church was started in 1845 as a kind of church for misfits in the area. They didn't look like misfits, but they kind of were. Zelienople, the town the church was "sort of" in—actually, we were in the town of Harmony, but Zelienople was the address—was founded in 1803 by a German Lutheran immigrant named Count Detmar Bassie. He bought 10,000 acres in the area and laid out the town. He named it after his daughter, Zelie.

A few years later, he sold half of the acreage to a leader of a splinter Lutheran sect named George Rapp. The sect was called the Harmonites. They had about 12,000 followers in Germany, but they were persecuted because of their beliefs and because Rapp was an illegal Lutheran lay preacher, which was a crime then. He was able to convince only about a thousand people or so to join him here in the US. He was a self-styled prophet who predicted Jesus would return in fall of 1829.

Ten years later, the Harmonites sold their acreage at a huge profit to a group of German Mennonites coming down from the Lehigh Valley. By the way, look up the Harmonites. They had an interesting history and set of beliefs. After them, other German immigrants came into the area and created a German Reformed Church, St. Peter's Reformed Church.

Anyway, what you're hearing in my story is a theme. Germans, Germans, Germans. Everyone in the area predominantly spoke German. In the early 1800s, the Lutherans did build an English Lutheran church to reach out to the second and third generation, as well as newcomers to the area, who spoke English. But some people in the community just didn't like the Lutheran, Mennonite, or German Reformed traditions. They didn't feel like they fit in. So they created what was then the Zelienople-Harmony United Presbyterian Church to be a church for the English- and Scottish-descent misfits in the area.

This history helped me realize the church started as an outlier, and that was part of their identity. That doesn't mean it was just some kind of rebel church. For a long time, prominent business people in the community had been part of the church, so it became an establishment church. But it always maintained something of an outlier mentality. I built on that context.

I've always been a bit of a misfit myself. I don't fit neatly into church categories because of my education and training in counseling and spiritual formation. I look at church differently. So, I decided to emphasize how we're different from other churches. I preached periodically that we were people who didn't fit with other churches and we're a church of people who have felt like misfits, who have been hurt by other churches, or who had simply walked away from other churches. I used the church's DNA to grow. And I told the church members Calvin's history in the process. In essence, I took my own ministry and molded it to the church's context.

Beth: How? How did you mold it?

Graham: Bluntly, I started saying to people we were a church of misfits. I sometimes joked we were like the Island of Misfit Toys from *Rudolph the Red-Nosed Reindeer*. We were more progressive than other churches in town, although that was relative. Those churches ranged from conservative evangelical to fundamentalist, so anything left of right seemed progressive. In truth, we were moderate. But I played up the criticism from other churches. I'd heard other

Christians in town called us the "church of sinners." So, I would say to people, "Other churches call us the 'church of sinners.' Well, what better place is there, then, to help people who feel like their lives have fallen apart? Aren't we all supposed to be churches for sinners"?

We emphasized in our literature we weren't like other churches because we emphasized love, compassion, and God's unconditional love. I emphasized the spiritual, saying we were a church where people could find God and we were a place for people who had been "spiritual, but not religious" and were willing to be "spiritual *and* religious." We started adding elements of worship unique to us, like Taizé chants, silence, communion every Sunday in one service, offering wine and grape juice during communion, and a whole variety of musical styles. We took our DNA and built on it. We became a misfit church again, but in a twenty-first-century way.

Ultimately, you aren't trying to recreate the church's origin, but you are trying to build on an origin and history that's already in place. I've noticed over the years that churches develop a certain character that's grounded in their origins. When we come in and treat them as though they're a blank slate, we end up automatically creating resistance because we're not taking into account who they already are.

If you want a church that's rooted in your vision for the church and your own DNA, you have to plant one. Until then, you're leading a church that's already been there, probably for over a hundred years. So, knowing its history helps you understand what it can do and be, and even more, what it can't do or be.

Beth: I hadn't thought about all of that. I'm not sure what to do with all of that. So, what would my church be?

Graham: I can't answer that because I don't know your church's history. But I can help you figure it out. It really comes down to understanding the *why* of your church.

Beth: The "why"?

Graham: Yeah. This isn't a concept that's all my own, although it is something I did intuitively from the beginning of my ministry. I think for me it comes from my counselor training, where we try to

39

understand the roots of things. Anyway, there's an organizational researcher named Simon Sinek who has written a book called *Start with Why*.[1] He became popular after his TED Talk of the same name.[2] His whole thesis is organizations fail over time because they only know *what* they do and *how* they do it, but lose sight of *why* they did things originally. They lose their sense of original purpose.

Actually, what he writes about is all part of what I call my "generational loss theory."

Beth: What's that?

Graham: It explains why our churches love our polities and traditions but aren't sure what to do with genuine God experiences. I think a significant reason for the decline of many denominational movements and churches is the loss of "why." In the beginning, the founder of a spiritual/religious movement, group, or sect has a compelling transforming vision with a loose organization around it to help others follow. The founder knows how to help people have this experience of God and so shares that vision and experience, as well as some of the ways to spread that experience. They offer a new spirituality that leads to more-direct experiences of God. Think St. Patrick of Ireland, St. Francis, Martin Luther, John Calvin, Menno Simons, George Fox, and, of course, John Wesley. These were founders who desperately wanted people to experience God through a unique approach to prayer, scripture, worship, and community.

Typically, a younger generation of followers loves that vision and these experiences, and so it tries to figure out ways to structure it so others can more consistently experience the same things. They create standardized ways of praying, reading, meeting, speaking, and the like. The third generation knows of the experiences, but it really falls in love with the structures of the experiences. Slowly, the experiences become less and less important, and the structure becomes more and more important. So, we get functional churches where people never experience God much, and eventually people start to walk away. Presently, we're in the umpteenth generation of mainline Protestant traditions, and in many cases, most of the things we emphasize are traditions, polities, and musical and preaching styles rooted in bygone days when these forms of worship led to deeper experiences. We've fallen in love with the form of our faith rather than with the original experience. Thus, people walk away. Nowadays, they are likely to call themselves "spiritual, but not religious," "nones," or "dones."

What happens is the founding "why," the founding passionate idea (or what we often call the "charism"), gets lost in the focus on structure. We become totally focused on *what* we are supposed to do and *how* we're supposed to do it. But we lose that original *why*—the reason why the founders were so passionate, and what they experienced and shared.

What we're left with is the structure of the founding experience without the experience itself. So, you get a Presbyterian movement that basically describes what and how we do things, rather than a movement based on the founding spiritual passion. The name "Presbyterian" is built on the Greek word, *presbyter*, which means "elder." To be a Presbyterian literally means to be part of a church run by elders. This doesn't capture our founding *why*, only our *what* and *how*. It says how we make decisions and what the process is. There's nothing in it about our approach to experiencing God. Lutherans are described as those who follow Luther's structure and theology but not necessarily his spirituality. Same with Episcopalians, whose name literally means they have bishops. And of course, you have the best name of all—Methodists, who follow Wesley's "method."

Beth: Okay, so I'm nailed as a follower of a "method." How do I figure out my and my church's "why"?

Graham: Look into the golden age of your church and its beginning. Explore their sense of their "golden age" first. Then explore why it was started, what its original vision and focus was. Even explore why your church had a resurgence some years ago under the previous pastor. How did he tap into the original why of the church?

Beth: You know, as you were talking, I started remembering more and more about my church. My church was founded in the 1870s. Back then, our town wasn't a suburb. It was a farming community. I'm not sure who founded it, but I think it was either first- or second-generation people from Ireland. I've seen pictures of people coming to church in the late 1800s, and I think they had names like Boyle and Denny and Shea.

There were pictures hanging in a church hallway that showed many people on horses and sitting in buggies in what's now the church parking lot. I asked a member about them. She said it was all the farming families coming to church on Sundays. Apparently, they used to ride their horses and buggies to church, and they'd bring food with them. After church, they'd have lunch together. And here's the amazing thing: they would have a second worship service in the afternoon. No football—worship. So, they'd go to worship twice on Sundays.

Graham: Ahhhh . . . I pine for the good old days when we pastors got to preach not one, but two two-hour sermons!

Beth: I'm sure that was it, although it's hard enough for me to preach now. That would scare me. Anyway, now that I think of it, I think my church was a farm church. Can that be a DNA?

Graham: Yeah, it's a DNA. And it may be why your church has a hard time doing suburban things. I realize all your members are suburbanites, but they've been going to a church with a farming DNA, and many chose that church to be their church. Let me ask you some questions. Do they tend to hang out for coffee afterward?

Beth: Actually, yes. In fact, they'll hang out for an hour after church just chatting. Also, we do a greeting time in worship to pass the peace and say hi to each other. You can't get them to stop. I quit trying a long time ago.

Graham: They're a country farm church, and farmers like to chat. What kind of mission do they like to do?

Beth: That's been a hard thing, getting them to do mission. I've tried to get them interested in overseas mission or even Methodist ministries. Not much enthusiasm.

Graham: Right, but what *do* they do?

Beth: They love giving food to the local food cupboard, and they like to give food to families in times of crisis or struggle. They're also good at responding to a crisis if there's flooding or fire or something like that. They will come out in droves during a crisis.

Graham: You've got a farm church. And for forever, they've been attracting farm personalities, even in a suburban area. That doesn't mean they're not suburban. It simply means deep down they have farm roots and will be attracted to farm-type ministries and missions updated for the twenty-first century. This idea of sustaining origins fits with my previous church. We were attracted to misfit ministries, to being a place for people who just don't completely fit in—hosting a community choir, offering rehearsal space for a jazz band, starting an afternoon program for teens, hosting singles dances for middle-aged singles, collecting bikes for a mission to South Dakota Native Americans, serving the food cupboard, building a labyrinth, and so much more.

Beth: How is a community choir something that doesn't fit in?

Graham: It's that choir in particular. They have over forty-five members, a number of whom have walked away from churches that had conflict or where they felt hurt. Also, it includes people from a variety of churches, people who might not connect with each other because of different theological perspectives. It also plays a wide variety of music that may or may not fit in churches, although nothing profane.

Okay, so let's get back to your church. Let's stay with the idea it's a farm church in a suburban area. What could that mean in terms of its ministry and mission?

Beth: I think it may influence us to be more traditional and cling to that. They generally look backward instead of forward. They will talk about how they used to be, and it's really difficult to get them to talk about what they could be. When they think about the large, growing, nondenominational churches in the area, they tend to do so critically. They look down their noses at them, talking about how shallow they are. I generally agree with them, but it also bugs me because I think our folks are shallow too. They won't engage in spiritual programs that bring depth, and they won't really engage in deeper, broader missions.

Graham: So, they cling to traditional ways, which can be frustrating, but what does it also mean in terms of what they might be willing to do?

Beth: *That's* harder to figure out.

Graham: Yes, it is, but that's because you're looking positively at the changes other churches have made while looking negatively at your own. It's that cynical, dark virus creeping in. Think more positively about your own church and its potential. Regardless of what they cling to, what does it also open up?

Beth: Well, I suppose it opens up ministry and mission around food.

Graham: Yes! So instead of trying to get them to be what they aren't, tap into who they are. What could you get them to do around food, chattiness, and things that are kind of "farmy"?

Beth: Certainly the food cupboard, which they already do. I suppose creating meals for the homebound and people facing difficulty.

Graham: What about dinners to support mission? It means collecting money instead of doing the actual hands-on mission. Can you live with that? Sometimes, pastors complain about members who give money instead of doing the work.

Beth: They probably would love that, although I'm not sure I would. I don't know if I can give up all my evenings for dinners, nor can my body. I've already gained a lot of weight since I became a pastor, and all the food churches have doesn't help. It's like all they know how to cook is fattening food!

Graham: Oh, yeah. Why go to a bakery when you can just go to a church and get free home-baked cookies and stuff? I learned early on in ministry not to eat much at church dinners but to have a small dinner beforehand. Otherwise, you balloon. Still, it's stuff they *will* do that supports ministry and mission. There's also something there that can be built on. Dinners to support mission may also open up people's imaginations to do more mission outside of their comfort zones.

Also, I can't tell whether you also don't like the chattiness of dinners, but you don't have to. Let them be chatty. Just support it, even if you're not chatty like them. My sense is your predecessor was chatty, but he also let them be chatty. Don't fight it. Let them be who they are.

Beth: Right. I've already been thinking like that as we've talked. I've sort of crushed the things they love to push them to do the things I love. I think the thing is I'm not entirely sure how to take them back to being a farm church.

Graham: I don't think you have to move them back. Their DNA is as a farm church, but that doesn't mean that's all they can do. What it means is you have to take into consideration their DNA and history. Then you build on that. You don't try to wipe out their history. You build on it and bridge to other things. They're now suburban. How do you create a hybrid farm/suburban church?

Beth: I have to think about that. My head's swirling a bit right now. I think what I'm hearing is I have to start with what they're willing to do and build on that, because what they're willing to do is rooted in what you call their DNA. So, if they're comfortable with food, start with stuff around food.

Graham: Yes, but not only food. Include the kind of chatty generosity farmers typically would have. They typically would give the shirts off their backs, but they won't always go to Africa to give someone that shirt.

Beth: That makes sense. So, for instance, perhaps doing clothing drives or the "Soles for Jesus" shoe contribution ministry I saw at the car wash last week.

Graham: Yes. And you don't have to think up all the ideas. Let them have fun thinking up ideas. It means taking a different tack that looks for the good in what they're already doing and willing to do, rather than thinking they're bad for not doing more of what you want them to do.

Beth: Oh my, I hadn't thought of it that way—of me being upset at them for not doing what I want them to do.

Graham: Well, it does add another element I'm afraid to talk about because I don't want your head to swirl too much. But there is another dimension to this.

Beth: I'm sure there is. You already have me swirling. You might as well keep going.

Graham: Okay, here goes: You also have to become aware of your history and DNA, because ultimately your being a successful leader means you have to lead them to create a hybrid between what you see for them and what they are willing to do. It's not you capitulating to them or them capitulating to you, which is what happens in far too many stubborn churches with stubborn pastors. You have to find a way to hold onto what you think is key for your vision while honoring and nurturing what they see as key. So, let's take a look at your history and DNA. Tell me about your church experiences growing up.

Beth: This is part of what has my head spinning. I grew up in a traditional, old, big church in a small county seat city. We had a big organ, pastors and choirs with robes, lots of formality. I both loved it and hated it. We also were a church that did a lot of mission, although a lot of it was giving money to support mission, such as rebuilding housing in the area, hosting a preschool, supporting a seminary, sponsoring several missionaries, and doing youth mission trips to rebuild places in West Virginia and Kentucky.

We also had these pastors who looked so imposing. The pastor during my junior and senior high school years was this booming man who spoke with so much authority. We had a youth pastor who was all energetic but also a bit too attracted to the girls. I don't think he ever did anything bad, but he certainly strutted when he was with mostly girls. With the guys, he acted a bit like a jock.

I think I got from my home church that mission was either building things for the poor or supporting mission stuff in other countries.

You know, I've been pretty influenced by the church where I was an associate pastor. It was a big, growing church. We had a large staff. There, I was in charge of family ministries, which was a glorified way of saying that I was in charge of youth groups and making sure the parents were on board.

Graham: And here comes the virus.

Beth: Sorry, I was in charge of family ministries. They were all so active, and we had so many things going on that now I feel like a failure if we don't have that much going on. In other words, I have this constant anxiety that if you have time on your hands, you're not doing ministry right. Makes me now wonder what Jesus did all the time, because he certainly didn't heal people and preach for eight hours a day. I think I've been having guilt over not being busier.

So, how have these churches' DNAs messed me up? I haven't been trying to recreate my previous churches, but I haven't *not* tried to recreate my previous churches. I think I'm trying to recreate something of my church married to the visions we got in seminary. In seminary, they talked so much about us being missional and getting out into the communities and doing all sorts of stuff everywhere that all I see is what we aren't doing.

Graham: What I hear you saying is you feel a bit like a failure in your church because they aren't doing the big mission of the church you grew up in, nor the kind you experienced in your previous church, nor the kind of work you learned in seminary that you're supposed to do. So the bar isn't just set high, but it's set over there instead of where you are.

Beth: What do you mean by "it's set over there"?

Graham: They set the bar by assuming that to be successful, you have to be like one of those churches you read about.

Beth: Oh yeah, and I'm not hitting those bars.

Graham: Which makes you feel like you're failing.

Beth: Yep.

Graham: You're not. From what you've told me, you're actually doing well. It sounds like from our previous sessions you're doing a good job of caring about them, letting them know they matter, and attending to them. I feel like I'm talking to the scarecrow from *The Wizard of Oz*: "You've had brains all the time. What you're missing is a diploma."

Well, what you're really missing is the sense that what you're doing is okay—something to validate that you are doing a good job. You have what I call "Willow Creek envy." That's when you look at all these other "successful" churches and measure yourself against them. You become competitive and think the only way you can be successful is to have this incredibly thriving church that is frenetic with activity. But what if that's not why God called you there? What if you aren't supposed to create a new Willow Creek?

So, I have a question: did Willow Creek have to figure out what their DNA was? They were a new church built in new suburbs atop old farmland. They were never a farm church. They were a church for people moving into newly built, transient, suburban areas. They got to create from scratch who they were. That's not your calling.

What if you're supposed to simply be for these people the pastor God wants you to be? What if you're called to affirm who they are while gently but firmly moving them into what they can be without losing who they are?

God called you here, not to Willow Creek, Saddleback, Hot Metal Community, Light Bulb Church, Coffee Community Church, or any of a million other churches built from scratch.

So, my biggest question for your swirly head is, can you be content with who you are, who they are, and where you are? Can you be content to create what you were called to create there, rather than trying to recreate something else there?

Beth: Oh my God . . . I don't know. Yes, I am envious. This isn't where I thought I'd be, coming out of seminary. I thought I'd have an easier time.

Graham: So does everyone. But the reality is all of us have been pastoring churches in some level of decline. Your church had a resurgence in the past, but it's now in a decline. Every pastor I'm working with has some level of envy that also has led them to feel like a bit of a failure. But that's because we keep measuring our success and failure against those big churches that started from scratch in high-growth, transient areas. How many of us are actually in those churches? Can you be the unique pastor called to your church and measure your success in terms of relationships, compassion, and service rather than attendance, membership, and frenetic activity?

Beth: That requires a shift in thinking. It's hard to make that shift because everything in my past says these aren't the right ways to measure success. But they also make more sense to me. I know I've been measuring myself against numbers, other churches, other pastors. Some of them have been the *big* evangelical or quirky emergent churches, but a lot of them have been the "other" churches in our conference. I keep reading in our denominational materials about all these great churches doing great things everywhere, and I think I get angry. I'm not one of them, but I want to be. I think what you're saying is that I don't have to be.

Graham: My foundational thought is God doesn't measure success by numbers. My sense is God measures success in terms of relationships and love. Can you tap into your church's love?

Beth: Probably. I think I'd have to rethink them and find a way to love them, rather than be disappointed with them.

Graham: *True dat.* So, let's simplify everything we've been talking about. It all starts with better understanding who they are at their roots and then understanding who you are. Then it means letting a hybrid church emerge that marries what you envision with what they will do.

Beth: Are there other pastors you're working with who are struggling to figure out their church's DNA?

Graham: All of them are to some extent. I have one pastor who leads two churches. We figured out one of his churches is a "frontier" church, having been created in the late 1700s on what was the frontier. Their DNA was being a church that only did things on Sundays, because that's what frontier people did. They eked out a living during the week and trekked to church on Sundays for the whole day. His frustration was they wouldn't do things during the week. So, he shifted most of the church activities to Sundays. His other church was a farm church like yours, but it's still in a farming community. So, he shifted to food and support ministries and missions for them. He still pushes them to do new things in both but began treating them differently.

I work with another pastor who's the pastor of a church that split twenty years ago. We call it a Horcrux[3] church because it feels like part of the church's soul is missing. So, his work is on helping them recover their soul.

Another pastor serves a merged church, which means it actually has two DNAs. So, we've worked on figuring out what it means to have a spliced DNA. She has had to search for both churches' DNAs and how they converge, while still creating space for ministries and mission that honor where they're different.

The point is ministry today is really hard because we're either in churches planted in older community contexts and have to adapt them to a new community and era, churches that exist in their unique bubbles, or churches that have complex DNA. It's much easier to start a new church based on our personal DNAs, but that's not our calling. We're called to pastor in the reality of the context we're in.

Beth: I hear you . . . and now I'm full!

Graham: Ha! Yes, you are. So, let's end here. I have an exercise for you to do between now and next time that might help.

FURTHER THOUGHTS

All of us who pastor in established churches face a significant advantage and disadvantage. The advantage is we're in churches where there's at least an established legacy of paying for professional pastors. Members *want* to be led by pastors, even if they resist. And they do give to the church.

We often don't consider this, but when churches give us pastors a salary, as well as pay for music directors, youth directors, office managers, bookkeepers, and the like, they're already doing ministry and mission. I realized a long time ago that a pastor's salary is ministry and mission. When we visit, counsel, write, serve, reach out, teach, preach, and lead, we are doing ministry and mission. And members' giving supports that. Never discount that. We can complain that all they do is write checks (or give online); but through us, they are caring for others. They are asking us pastors to do what they can't, which is to do what we're skilled in doing. In essence, when they give to the church, they're asking us to be their hands and feet in work they don't feel competent to do.

The disadvantage of serving an established congregation is we have to adapt to where we are, and often we aren't trained in doing that. Just as churches have baggage, so do we. If we loved or liked the church of our youth, then we will want to emulate that to some extent. If we had a bad experience in a church of our youth or even of our adulthood, we will try to correct that. We also come with theological and spiritual convictions that may be at odds with the church we are called to lead. Our theology might not be fully compatible with their theological DNA. What do we do then? If we are on fire for social justice in an area where traditional values reign, what do we do? How do we fit ourselves to where we are? We have to consider all of that.

We often think of churches as blank slates we can lead to accomplish our vision, but the reality is they aren't. They have a history that needs to be honored. That history is the soil out of which they can grow new fruit. We can't just assume any seed will work. We have to be careful about what we plant and how we nourish. You don't plant a beautiful cactus in good soil with plenty of water, and you don't plant a flowering apple tree in desert sand.

Figuring out both a church's DNA and our own is hard work because we both resist introspection. Churches often don't write their histories; or if they do, they don't do it very well. So we have to become quasi-historians who do what we can to uncover history. This requires spending time with older members to find out what they know of the church's history. A by-product of meeting with older members is it also bonds us with them and creates the conditions where they enhance their support of our ministries. I spent a lot of time in my early years at Calvin Presbyterian Church talking with these older members, and they became some of the church members I was most fond of and still miss the most now.

Figuring out our own DNA is also hard because it might require working with a therapist, spiritual director, coach, or mentor who is adept at helping us understand ourselves. It means figuring out where our wounds are, what our unrealistic expectations are, and what our baggage is. But the clearer we are on these, the better we become at being *intentional* leaders who lead churches to what God is calling them to be. We're able to lead them away from what they want to anxiously cling to while resisting the urge to force them to become something they really can't be.

So what questions do we ask to uncover a church's and our own DNA? The following exercise might help.

CHURCH AND PERSONAL DNA EXERCISE

Explore your congregation's DNA.

A) Investigate your church's history. This investigation does not have to be an extensive deep dive. It just needs to be thorough enough for you to gain a sense of why your church was founded: who the original population of the church was (e.g., German immigrants, Scottish pioneers, a growing mining community, GIs starting young families, a community of summer Bible camps, a new hi-tech community, farmers, and so forth), what it emphasized when it was thriving, and what characteristics it had. This information can be gleaned in a combination of ways:

  1. *Read a printed history of the church or look through the church's historical documents.*
  2. *Talk with older, lifetime members who remember the musings of their parents and grandparents.*
  3. *Read printed local town or city histories.*
  4. *Look over original or early board minutes.*
  5. *Reflect on saved and stored early church pictures.*
  6. *Have conversations with previous pastors.*
  7. *Consider any other sources that promise to reveal the church's history.*

B) As you collect information, write short sentences about what you've found. For example, based on Calvin Presbyterian Church's past, these might be:

  1. *Area dominated by German Protestants.*
  2. *Started by families of English and Scottish descent who wanted their own kind of worship.*
  3. *Initially called the Harmony-Zelienople United Presbyterian Church in 1845 and forced to adopt the name Calvin United Presbyterian Church in 1959 after a denominational merger. The church never liked the name because they never considered themselves "Calvinist" and because they were forced to adopt it.*
  4. *Other, more conservative churches in town called us "the church of sinners," which might be a good thing to build on.*

> 5. *The music director described the church as "not being a church for everyone," meaning people who want the church to fit a stereotype would be disappointed.*

C) Distill the sentences into short descriptions based on the histories collected. For example, Calvin Presbyterian Church was started by those of English and Scottish descent who didn't consider themselves "Calvinists" and were criticized by more conservative churches. The church was referred to as one that's not for everyone. Thus, it seemed like a church for "misfits," although other descriptions would similarly be valid—"Presbyterian roots"; "an alternative church"; or something similar.

D) Develop a descriptive statement for your church that is rooted in its DNA. It may go something like this:

"Originally founded as a church for _____ [insert demographic], _____ [insert name of your church] is now a community striving to _____ [verb]."

- For example, "Originally founded as a church for farmers, Farm Community Church is now a community striving to spiritually, psychologically, and physically feed those in the community."

Simultaneously explore your DNA.

A) Take time to explore your own faith and church history. Gain a sense of what aspects of church, ministry, and mission have attracted you. More importantly, explore why they have attracted you.

B) As you explore your background information, write short sentences about what's been important to you. For example, these might be:

> 1. *I've been influenced by my home church, which had both traditional and contemporary worship services.*
>
> 2. *I'm attracted to overseas mission, such as in Malawi or Ghana.*
>
> 3. *I love small groups and Bible studies.*

C) Distill the sentences into a short description of what's in your faith DNA. For example, based on the above you could write, "I love churches that can go deep and reach out."

D) Develop a descriptive statement for yourself that is rooted in your DNA. It may go something like this:

"My deepest passion is to _____, which I feel most deeply when I _____."

Synthesize both statements into a statement that honors both your own and your church's histories and DNA.

A) Synthesize your own personal statement with the church's in a way that allows you and the church to share a vision:

"Rooted in a passion for _____ [insert common mission/ministry], _____ [insert name of your church] is a community striving to _____ [verb]."

- For example, "Rooted in a passion for feeding others, Farm Community Church is a community striving to feed bodies and souls here and throughout the world."

B) Distill this down even more by focusing on the key words:

- Key words from previous sentence: "rooted in passion," "feeding others," "community," "feed bodies and souls," "here and throughout the world."
- Thus, "Farm Community Church: Feeding bodies and souls, here and throughout the world."

This can become a guiding statement rooted in the church's and our own DNA.

NOTES

1. Simon Sinek, *Start with Why: How Great Leaders Inspire Everyone to Take Action* (New York: Penguin, 2009).

2. Simon Sinek, "Start with Why: How Great Leaders Inspire Action," lecture, TEDxPugetSound, September 8, 2009, Puget Sound, WA, video, 18:01, https://tinyurl.com/jdrfgxy.

3. The term *Horcrux* comes from the *Harry Potter* series of books and films by J. K. Rowling. A Horcrux is an item in which the main antagonist, Voldemort, has hidden a piece of his soul so he can have an immortal life. The only way to slice off that piece of soul is to engage in a violent act of murder that tears the soul, making it available for hiding. In the series, Voldemort has committed seven murders, allowing pieces of his soul to be placed in seven different objects or creatures.

3

RESISTING
RELATIONSHIPS

Alan is a Presbyterian pastor of a suburban church in Pennsylvania that's in an area with a relatively stable population. He's been the solo pastor of his current church for a little over three years. He accepted the call there after serving a similar church in a suburb of Columbus, Ohio. He left there after feeling frustrated with the church and its apparent unwillingness to make his suggested changes. His current church has been either stagnant or in decline for about fifteen years, and it has become a primarily older congregation, although there are some younger families. In their search for a new pastor, the church emphasized its desire to grow and its willingness to make changes.

Alan has slowly become more frustrated with ministry in general and this church in particular. The combination of his previous experiences and the unexpected, growing resistance in this church causes him to feel like a failure. He entered spiritual direction and coaching because he was beginning to wonder if he was truly called to ministry.

We had previously met five times. He came to this particular session wearing jeans and a sweatshirt, which is a bit different from his usual, more formal attire.

****

Graham: Wow, sweatshirt. It looks like a comfort day today.

Alan: Yeah, I felt a bit down and just wanted to wear more comfortable clothes.

Graham: Down because of the same stuff we talked about last time—about the church and its resistance to your ministry?

Alan: Yeah, I think something happened in me this past week that drained my energy.

Graham: Something specific?

Alan: I don't know. There's nothing I can point to. It's more like I just started to get tired and didn't want to do any of the things I normally like to do. I just felt like staying home and having a Netflix binge. But even then I wasn't sure what to do. I had Netflix on last night and spent literally forty-five minutes trying to find a program to watch that would make me feel better. I never really settled on anything.

Graham: Is that kind of a metaphor for where you are right now—scanning and looking but never really settling on anything?

Alan: It has been recently. I have no idea what to do with my church anymore, and I know I sound like a broken record since we talked about this the last two times we met. I'm wondering if I've developed a pattern. I come into a church thinking I'll turn the place around, that I'll be their savior. They pretend to want all my new ideas when all they really want is a guy in a robe on Sunday mornings. I start throwing out all my best ideas at them. They shoot them down one at a time. I'm left scanning for something to do. And then I start thinking about leaving.

Graham: So, you're thinking about leaving.

Alan: I dunno. Maybe. Kind of. I'm just so disappointed right now. I thought I could make a difference. I got into ministry to make a difference. I'm not making much of a difference. I'm a guy in a robe on Sundays. I even get people on Sundays saying to me, "That was a really good sermon, Alan. I really liked it." All I can think is, "Do you lie to your husband like that?"

Graham: So, right now you're a Bad Luck Schleprock.

Alan: A *whaaa?*

Graham: A Bad Luck Schleprock. He was a character in a really bad cartoon from my childhood. For a couple of years in the early 1970s, there was a sequel to *The Flintstones* cartoon called *The Pebbles and Bamm-Bamm Show*. It starred the babies from *The Flintstones*, Pebbles and Bamm-Bamm, as teenagers in high school. One of their friends was named Blackrock Schleprock. He was sort of like Eeyore from *Winnie the Pooh*. He literally walked around hunched over with a dark gray raincloud hovering above, muttering things like, "Nothing ever will ever be good again." That seems like where you are right now.

Alan: So, for us younger folks, you're telling me I'm becoming like Eeyore.

Graham: Yes, and that would have saved us some time, although Pooh actually came before my time. I'll try again: So, right now you feel like Eeyore.

Alan: Yes, it feels like nothing good is ever going to happen again.

Graham: What's really getting you down is your having a passion for ministry and for them, and then they resist everything you suggest.

Alan: Yeah, or almost everything.

Graham: So, there have been some things they've adopted.

Alan: Some things, but not many.

Graham: What's worked?

Alan: We bought our denomination's new hymnals. So, we're now trying some new songs.

Graham: Okay. That's interesting, since churches often resist new songs. How did you get them to go along with that?

Alan: Yeah, um . . . well, it started with the choir director telling me she thought we should get the new hymnal.

Graham: So, you did?

Alan: Not right away. She and I talked and decided to create a small task force of choir members to look at the hymnal.

Graham: And?

Alan: Oh, you want more detail?

Graham: Yeah, I want to hear about the process.

Alan: Oh, okay. We started the task force. We asked three choir members to work with the music director, Sue, to go through it and see what they thought about the hymns. Over two months, they met for an hour before choir practice. Some of the other choir members joined them. Sue already had left out hymns she knew the choir either would have a tough time singing or that just seemed too old. Sue's good at letting go of old stuff and being open to new stuff without being too radical. She's good at getting people to work together on songs.

Graham: My guess is they had a good time doing this.

Alan: I think they did. I heard laughter from their group periodically when I was there on Wednesday evenings.

Graham: So, then what happened?

Alan: Once they had done their review of the hymnal, they shared some of the newer songs with the choir to show them. The choir really got behind it. So, we had Sue and one of the choir members come to a session meeting to explain their recommendation. Afterward, the session voted unanimously to invite the congregation to contribute to the new hymnals.

Graham: Was it just a letter or something else?

Alan: Oh, we sent out a letter, put it in our bulletin and newsletter, and some of the task force members gave an announcement.

Graham: Did people give reluctantly?

Alan: No, not at all. In fact, within two weeks we had received enough contributions to buy way more hymnals than we needed.

Graham: Wow! That's so cool. Let's come back to this in a bit. I want to steer you in a different direction. So, that was one thing that went well. Normally, what does the resistance to what you want to do look like?

Alan: Oh crap! You still want to talk about *that*? Sometimes, it's the shitty—sorry—*crappy* statement in the shake-hands line after a sermon: "Pastor, what made you decide to preach *that* on a communion Sunday?" or "Not one of your best sermons, Alan." Sometimes, I get anonymous letters, although I can often figure out who sent them. Other times, it's someone in a meeting who just says out loud they don't like my idea and it would take us in the wrong direction.

Graham: Was their criticism like this at first?

Alan: No, it grew over time. At first, they all seemed energetic about my ideas. Then, it was like someone flipped a switch overnight about a year ago. It actually seemed to start in a worship committee meeting when I suggested we do something from your book *In God's Presence*.[1] I suggested we start worship off with a Taizé chant instead of the printed call to worship.

Graham: Yikes! I caused your conflict? Sorry.

Alan: It wasn't you. It was like they just got tired of my ideas. Since then, it's been like pulling teeth.

Graham: So, what do you think they're saying to you through all this resistance?

Alan: They don't want to change!

Graham: I don't think that's what they're saying. I think that's just what you *think* they're saying.

Alan: Then I don't know what they're saying.

Graham: (smiling and chuckling) Now *you're* just resisting change.

Alan: What do you mean?

Graham: I'm pushing you ever so slightly to change your thinking about them and to look at things through their eyes. What do you think they're saying to you? They went along with you for a while, and they certainly went along with Sue. So, what do you think they're trying to tell you when they resist?

Alan: Can you give me some help on this?

Graham: Sure. Let's take a step back. When you used my book with them, you were trying to get them to look at worship differently, right?

Alan: Yeah.

Graham: And they were okay with that for a while, right?

Alan: Yep.

Graham: And then there was one suggestion too far.

Alan: I didn't think about it that way. Yeah, it was one suggestion too far.

Graham: Had you been making a lot of suggestions?

Alan: Well, the book was making suggestions, and I think I was pushing them to hurry up and change things.

Graham: "Hurry up." "Change things." So, I'll ask my question from earlier: What do you think they're trying to tell you when they resist?

Alan: I think they're saying I'm pushing them too hard.

Graham: So, why are you pushing so hard?

Alan: I want them to grow and to be successful.

Graham: Why are you pushing them to grow and be successful?

Alan: Shouldn't all of us want our churches to grow and be successful?

Graham: Ahhh . . . resistance. Dig deeper. Why do *you* want them to grow and be successful?

Alan: I don't know. Maybe so I'll be seen as successful.

Graham: Now we're getting somewhere. They're not moving fast enough for you. You have a schedule for success, and they're not keeping up with it. How do you get them back on your schedule?

Alan: (chuckling) I know, right? So, what do I do?

Graham: Well, the problem is they're resisting you, and so you have to become a therapist with their resistance.

Alan: A therapist with their resistance?

Graham: Yuh! Okay, I'm about to let you peek into the secret life of therapists, into the secret world of things we know that we've sworn never to reveal. (smiling) To be a therapist is to constantly overcome resistance. That's what we always work with. In any therapy, spiritual direction, or coaching session, our clients will always resist us at some point. Those of us who are any good know how to overcome resistance, so the resistance doesn't grow to become a defense mechanism. There's something of a progression when it comes to how people protect their cherished ideas, values, and traditions. At first, they resist an idea by ignoring it, pushing back against it, or criticizing it. If we continue to push them, then their resistance turns into a defense mechanism such as denial, projection, regression, generalizing, anger, and a bunch of others. Defense mechanisms are resistances that have become concrete. They become walls we build to defend ourselves from all possible threats. Resistance is merely the first bricks of a wall, so there's a possibility we can gently pull them away. Once resistance turns to a defense, we lose our ability to sway them because they will no longer listen to us.

Once a client becomes defensive, the resistance has won. In your church, once they become defensive, it's really hard to overcome it. Your particular church has shifted from being resistant to becoming defensive. They're defending against your ideas. How do you tell if they've become defensive rather than resistant? They're becoming more passive-aggressive, covert-aggressive, and just plain aggressive, which are all hallmarks of defensive behavior. A resistant person only mildly does these. Defensive people do them all the time.

Alan: Covert-aggressive?

Graham: Passive-aggressive's little brother. It's when you do something that is actually aggressive, but you can deny it by pretending it is normal. For example, being irritated with your wife about something, and then, while she's getting dressed saying, "You're not going to wear that!" When she gets angry back, you just say, "Hey, I'm just trying to keep you from being embarrassed at work." You're aggressive, but you pretend you're not. Anyway, that's off the topic. The point is once your church becomes defensive, which I think yours has, the resistance has won.

Alan: So, what do I do?

Graham: Is it okay if I talk about resistance for a while and teach you more about it?

Alan: Actually, that would be great.

Graham: The first thing to realize is everything is about relationships—church, worship, meetings, ideas, budgets—no matter what we're talking about in the church, it's about relationships. When people resist us, it means the relationship has started to get uncomfortable. You already know this in your family. If you come down to breakfast in the morning armed with a bundle of great ideas for the family for the day, what's their first response to all your ideas?

Alan: They say, "Dad, drink your coffee and chill!"

Graham: Right, because they're *resisting* you.

Alan: And Dad's a dweeb.

Graham: Especially that for all of us dads. In fact, one of my main tasks in life is to be the resident dweeb at home!

Back to resistance. There's a wonderful book about transforming organizations called *Switch*, by two brothers, Chip and Dan Heath.[2]

They use a metaphor they call "the elephant" for an organization's emotional resistance. It's part of a larger metaphor for transforming organizations, which they say is a process of trying to get a rider to ride an elephant down a path. The rider is the rational part of the organization. The path is the vision we want for the organization. If we try to get a rider to ride an elephant down a path, we would typically point out the path to the rider through rational arguments and then try to convince him or her to ride the elephant down the path. Seems like a rational, normal thing to do, right?

Alan: Yeah.

Graham: But there's one problem: what if the elephant doesn't want to go down the path? How do you get it to go down?

Alan: I dunno . . . smack its bum?

Graham: Do you want to smack an elephant's bum? You'd probably end up dead. That's the problem. We think the rational rider's in charge and the visionary path is obvious. We don't take into account what the elephant sees and wants. What if the elephant's scared? What if the elephant is tired? What if the elephant is complacent? The elephant is the emotional life of your congregation. You can make rational arguments all you want to the rider, and you can make visionary statements all you want about the path; but if the elephant doesn't feel safe or it doesn't feel like it can trust your rationale, it's not going down the path. This last point's the most important. If the elephant doesn't trust you, you ain't going nowhere.

Alan: So, you're saying the congregation doesn't trust me?

Graham: I'm saying resistance is about fear, distrust, and confusion. To overcome resistance, you have to get people to feel safe, trust you, and have a sense they know what the outcome will be. When a church resists your ideas, they are saying that they either don't feel safe, don't trust you, or are confused—or all three. Let's go back to your idea about the Taizé chant. You pushed them, and they then became the elephant that just sat down and wouldn't move. They didn't feel safe because they might have felt bullied or worried you'll leave them stuck with your idea as you move on to another congregation, or as though you're doing what a previous pastor did. You may not have spent enough time building up trust, especially if you came into the place armed with new ideas and not enough relationship building. Remember, it's all about relationships. They may feel you have an agenda other than their best interests and that you don't care about them. Or they may just be tired and confused about what the outcome will be and feel safer and better doing nothing and sticking with what they know.

Alan: Oh God. Do you think they think all that?

Graham: No, only the rider would think all that. The elephant would *feel* all that, and that's the difference. Elephants feel. They can feel calm, they can feel happy, but they can also feel threatened and scared and chaotic. And when they do, they start swinging their trunks at everything in sight. When churches do, we pastors can become victims of elephant stampedes.

Alan: Oh God!

Graham: It's not that hopeless. The elephants are *resistance*. Every good therapist understands resistance comes from fear or insecurity or anxiety or weak relationships that lead the elephant to be cautious and distrustful. Therapy is all about relationships and forging trust. Ministry and leading churches are all about relationships and trust too.

Relationships with the elephant are always built on an emotional connection, not rationale or vision. The rider and the path are secondary. So, all your rational arguments don't do the trick because the resistance is emotional, not intellectual. Also, it's very important to realize resistance is not sabotage. It's anxiety and fear that cause people to fight, flee, or freeze.

There are many ways to think about resistance. I'm going to get a bit wonky here, so I hope you'll bear with me.

Alan: Go ahead. I think I'm keeping up. I'm also glad I have a thirty-minute drive home to think about this stuff. Okay . . . wonky ways to overcome resistance.

Graham: Here goes . . . There are four therapeutic theories about why resistance occurs and combining the four gives us a fuller picture.[3]

The first way of understanding it comes from what's called *psychodynamic theory*. Basically, it sees resistance as an attempt by people

65

to control their anxiety. It says change is always anxiety-provoking, and resistance is an unconscious response to threats. It's not typically intentional. So, when it comes to our ideas, people resist because they're scared of our solutions to stagnation, but they don't really know they're anxious and afraid.

Cognitive theory looks at it a bit differently. It sees resistance as clients' negative or destructive thinking patterns that make change difficult. In other words, they've learned to think negatively about any change because they're suspicious it won't work, it will fail, or worse things will follow. Their thinking is set, and new thinking is a threat.

Behavioral theory sees resistance as the result of the wrong set of reinforcers rewarding change, *and* the wrong set of negative consequences allowing a person to remain unchanged. In other words, neither the rewards for changing nor the consequences for staying the same are strong enough. It's kind of the carrot-and-stick approach.

Social interaction theory sees resistance as the result of weak, negative, or dysfunctional relationships. Thus, with ministry, they might say resistance is the result of negative and weak relationships between the leaders of the church and the members, or between the pastor and the leaders.

So, ball all of this up, and it gives us a three-dimensional way of understanding resistance:

- People resist because they're anxious in the face of change.
- They resist because they aren't aware enough of the reality of their situation and have a hard time thinking through it all. So, they don't recognize that their decline and stagnation are a problem because the closed-system familiarity they have with each other feels like a good thing.
- They resist because the changes don't seem positive enough and staying the same doesn't seem negative enough. They don't realize bad things will happen if they don't change and good things can come from change.
- Our style of leadership doesn't lead to strong relationships,

which diminishes others' willingness to follow us. In essence, they don't feel close enough to us as pastors.

Okay, so that's a lot of things to think through. Hopefully, I'm not panicking your elephant by talking about all of this.

Alan: No, I'm following you, but I may need you to write this down for me.

Graham: Oh, I'll send you an email afterward with it, since I actually have this written down from a presentation I did. So, how do we put all of this together?

First, pastors facing resistance have failed to realize church members are always going to be initially ambivalent about *all* change. They may want it, but they also don't. So, they end up feeling anxious about even good change.

Second, we tend to want more for the church than the church wants for itself, meaning we end up working harder than the church. Also, we are clearer about what we want than they are, and the combination of us pushing our agenda and not helping them think through the changes works against the changes.

Third, we can become too intent on our personal agendas and become critical when they don't follow. So, we stop being positive and start becoming cynical, which they notice. They know we're irritated with them, so they start tuning us out.

Fourth, we try too hard to *fix* the church, and we end up pushing the church to go too fast. In the process, they begin to realize we're not as interested in a relationship with them as we are in *fixing* them. So, even more resistance arises because their response to our ideas leads us to feel inadequate, causing us to push harder or give up.

Here's another way of thinking about all of this. We can't actively change our churches by trying to change our churches. We can only change how we interact with our churches to bring about change. In essence, when we create positive relationships with them that help them feel safe and trust us, they follow. That's what happened with your hymnals.

The choir members and you trusted Sue. She created a process that included people she and the choir trusted to make a decision.

They entered a process that was fun and meaningful. They shared it with your board, whom the members trusted, and then the board and you shared it with the congregation. In the process, through the bulletin, newsletter, and announcements by trusted members, the elephants got excited about the idea. Your elephants were wanting to walk down the path to the new hymnals. All you had to do was jump on board and ride along.

Alan, here's the thing: we can't overcome resistance by trying harder. We only increase resistance when we do. The more we push them, the more they push back, which is what makes overcoming resistance so hard. When people resist, we generally push harder rationally to make our case and convince them to do what we want. We're too rider-focused, not elephant-focused. We think we can convince the elephant with rational arguments. We can't. We convince the elephants through trusting relationships.

Good therapists and good pastors recognize when people aren't responding to our pushes or when they are pushing back, it's a sign we're working too hard and not giving them space to process. So, we have to step back.

Alan: So, that's *all* we have to do? (rolls eyes) I'm only kidding. That's a lot to keep in mind.

Graham: Yeah, it is. That's why therapists take a long time to learn techniques for overcoming resistance. Licensed therapists have to do between 3,000 and 3,500 hours of clinical supervision with someone who understands this stuff. The sad part is in our training for ministry, most of us receive no training in overcoming resistance. In fact, many of those who teach church transformation tell you pain is part of change and you just have to push your way through it. That's fine if you have a high pain tolerance, but most pastors are pretty sensitive.

Alan: So, what do you do?

Graham: That's both the hard and easy part. There are ways of overcoming resistance. The number one, most important, certified-gold way of overcoming resistance is to *focus on reducing anxiety*. If you're being resisted, assume they're anxious and can't put a finger on why, other than it's you and your changes. So, assume they're anxious and look for ways to reduce anxiety. It may mean holding off on that change you want to do. It may mean doing a sermon on how anxious you are when making changes and what you do to overcome your anxiety spiritually, while also praising them for their ability to overcome their anxiety with your crazy ideas. It may mean spending more time visiting. It may mean spending time with the biggest resisters and listening to their struggles.

A second way of overcoming resistance is by making changes easier and simpler. This is difficult for all of us because we've been *cursed* by our knowledge and expertise. We've learned all sorts of things about church growth from bright teachers. Our members haven't. Usually, they're hearing things from you for the first time, and they haven't reflected on what you're trying to do. That one small step for you may seem like a giant leap for them.

I learned this by helping run a behavior modification program in a psychiatric hospital early in my career. The running mantra was behavior modification always works. If it's not working, it's because the steps we're asking them to take are too big. So, make the steps smaller and simpler. Same thing with church changes. They may actually want to change, but the steps of change or the pace of change may be too much for them. So, break things down into what are called *successive approximations*—smaller steps that accumulate over time like raindrops or bricks.

By the way, this isn't just me. There's a wonderful book out there called *Atomic Habits* by a guy named James Clear.[4] He talks about how changing habits begins with the smallest steps. You reduce anxiety by reducing the size of the steps and the pace of change. That's hard because it also increases *your* anxiety because you want to get things done quickly so you can be a more rapid success.

Finally, when resistance rises, focus on reestablishing trusting relationships and an ethos of trust throughout your church. You've heard me say many times that in the end, church is about relationships. You can make all sorts of changes, but if they don't enhance relationships between us and God, us and others, and us and ourselves, they really won't amount to much. Whatever changes you make, you need to emphasize the relational nature of them. And when resistance arises, you have to then put your attention on grow-ing trusting relationships in your church. This means trusting them more but also leading in a way that leads them to trust you more.

Alan: So, how have you done the last one, getting them to trust you more?

Graham: I'll give you a great example. Early on in my ministry at Calvin Church, we created another worship service that met at 8:30 a.m. As part of it, we did a very un-Presbyterian thing: we served communion every week in that service, and we reintroduced wine along with grape juice. We found people really liked having com-munion every week. In fact, many long-term, first-service worship-pers said they no longer liked going to our second service because there wasn't communion. This went against everything Presbyteri-ans tend to believe, which is if you do communion every week, it becomes less special. Congregants at this service found celebrating weekly made communion *more* special. When there was no commu-nion, they felt as though something was missing.

Knowing how powerful the experience of weekly communion was for them, we decided to try offering weekly communion in our sec-ond service. So, every Sunday we started having communion in our second service too. We did all the right things in reducing resistance; but when it came down to it, about 20 percent of the congregation at that service *hated* it. And they were very vocal about it. I really got tired of all the complaints, and with what I thought were lame rea-sons for wanting communion only once a month.

I intentionally spent time with several prominent resisters as I lis-tened to their arguments: "Having communion every week is like having prime rib every week. I love it, but it's too much." Or, "When there is communion every week it makes the service too long."

So, after two months, we ended the experiment. But we didn't stop there. I wrote a small letter that was inserted in the following Sunday's bulletin. It also became a small article in our newsletter. In it, I talked about how we tried to share the experiences from the first worship service. I talked about how much of a positive impact it made on them. Then I said we now realize the first service is a special service, and many who go to it are seeking weekly communion because it helps them sense God's presence. But we also recognize that for others, less frequent communion helps them sense God's presence. I then went on to say what makes our congregation so special is that members allow us to try these things and are really supportive and caring in doing so. I finally mentioned it's the willingness to try new things, and their patience with the process, that sets our members apart from other churches. I thanked them and said they are truly a special group of people.

Alan: So, you lied to them.

Graham: Not one bit. Everything I said was true. I didn't share my irritation, but I didn't need to. That wasn't the point. The point was they tried it for two months. I accentuated the positives of the experiment and the positives about the congregation. Remember, only about 20 percent were against it. Probably 50 percent were neutral, and 30 percent were positive. What we didn't consider when we tried the experiment is the 30 percent who always had the option of going to the first service. Meanwhile, the 20 percent had no other recourse other than walking away from Calvin Church for a church that offered only monthly communion.

But what you really need to hear is I helped them reduce future resistance, because now they knew we listened to them and valued their opinions. Even more, they learned they could trust us. Remember the path to reducing resistance is through enhancing relationships. Anytime there's long-term resistance, it's an indication of the state of your relationships with them.

Alan: I get that. And I think I've not paid as much attention to the relationships.

Graham: Do you mind if I ask you a tough question regarding you and your relationship with your church?

Alan: Probably . . .

Graham: So, don't ask it?

Alan: Oh no, ask it. I'll just probably mind. But that's not the same as saying you shouldn't ask. See? I'm figuring out my own resistance.

Graham: Okay, so here's my question: what are your members to you?

Alan: What do you mean?

Graham: In the end, for you, what's the purpose of your members for you?

Alan: They're God's children.

Graham: C'mon. No, they aren't. Or at least that's not what they are for you except in your best moments.

Alan: How can you say they aren't?

Graham: I'm not saying objectively they aren't, but that's not what they are to you. You talk about how disappointed you are with them because they won't grow the way you want them to, they won't do the ministry and mission programs you want them to do. So, be honest: what are they to you?

Alan: Crap! They may be widgets.

Graham: Widgets?

Alan: Yeah, widgets I want to produce so others will think I'm successful.

Graham: And perhaps get you to a better, bigger church down the road.

Alan: If I'm being brutally honest, yeah.

Graham: And that's why they resist you. They know that. They suspect you might leave if they're too successful. Remember that the pathway to success in ministry is always by increasing and enhancing relationships. If you relate to them as widgets, they'll resist relationships with you.

I'll also add one more thing: a church will always become what we pastors believe it is. So, if you believe they're flawed, they'll become very flawed. If you believe they're great, they'll become great. If they disappoint you, they'll become a disappointing congregation. If they please you, they'll become a pleasing one.

Alan: (slumping a bit in his chair) Ugh! So, how do I get out of all of this?

Graham: Work on your relationship with them and quit worrying about how they measure up. Kick your professors off your shoulders. Get rid of the folks who are standing there whispering to you that you have to preach a certain way, do more mission, be more prophetic, be more outward-looking, and be more . . . *more!* You don't have to get rid of all of them, but remember that your relationship is with your members, not your past professors. By the way, I'm not saying your professors were bad. I'm saying often in our training, we get so many voices from so many "experts" that we end up trying to serve their agendas rather than serving as we're called to serve. Hold onto what they taught that's relevant, and don't be afraid to let go of the rest.

Also, stop trying to earn stars in heaven and the accolades of your colleagues. Instead, focus on what God led you there to do. In the process, love them and nurture them. Be a pastor of a flock.

Alan: I can do that. Actually, I think this makes me feel better. I can care about them. It may even take pressure off. Instead of measuring me in terms of how much they are doing, measure my ministry in terms of how caring I am with them.

Graham: Yes. Oh, and I have one last thought to leave with you. Do you know how many pastors feel the way you have in all your frustrations? Almost all of them. You're not alone. So many pastors out there feel the same way you do. Unfortunately, they also share similar characteristics, too, because they keep trying to fix their churches instead of trying to love them. I had an insight long ago that every pastor who comes into a church, whether as an interim or regularly called pastor, thinks she or he has to *fix* the church from the previous pastor's ministry. If that's true, then all our churches become one patch atop another, atop another, atop another.

When I came to Calvin Presbyterian Church, I never tried to fix them. I loved a lot of what the previous pastor, Dick Anderson, did. He was a wonderful man and friend of mine. I simply tried to build on what he set as a foundation. He was mission-focused. I'm not as mission-minded as he was, or at least my sense of mission has revolved more around mental health and spiritual growth, but his influence was still there twenty-two years later because I just built on the foundation he set.

So, your assignment for the next week is to figure out how to love them more. Does this seem to be enough for this week?

Alan: More than enough. Thanks.

Graham: Good. Let's pray.

FURTHER THOUGHTS

The problem of resistance is perhaps the most ignored issue of pastoral leadership in the mainline Protestant church. It's a prevalent problem precisely because of the mainline Protestant church's decline. Many of our churches, if not most, have lost their younger, more risk-taking members, leaving us with members who tend to excel at loyalty and commitment but not at embracing possibility and change.

Many of our church members, and perhaps the majority of lay church leaders, often feel the pain of the changes sweeping through church culture. It can make them feel anxious and afraid. They're afraid of what the decline may mean in the end and are anxious that anything they try may fail, thus leading to a faster pace of decline.

Wonderful articles and books are being written about adaptive leadership and church transformation, but often their models come from organizational theory developed in the context of businesses where leaders and employees can be fired and replaced. How do you fire and replace a congregation and its leaders? I would be the first to admit I have been heavily influenced by organizational theory, but the therapist part of me also recognizes there's something else going on in the mainline Protestant church that is more akin to what I've seen as a therapist than as an organizational leader. Simply put, people who come to therapists for counseling are generally anxious, afraid, skeptical, and unsure whether to trust. The therapist has to consider this and create a delicate balance: develop a trusting relationship while nudging clients to go deeper and further. The further and deeper the therapist takes them, the more anxious they become. So, the therapist has to build a sense of trust as a foundation that helps clients gain courage.

The churches of mainline Protestant denominations are often similar to therapy clients. They've been plagued by their own survival fears, yet they still recognize their need to adapt, change, and reinvent themselves. The conflict often leaves them paralyzed. What they want is someone who they can trust who will say, "It's okay. You're all going to be okay." This isn't the message many pastors give to their churches. Often pastors have not been trained to create trusting relationships with their churches. They've been taught to be missional, prophetic, evangelical, adaptive, and transformational. What they're missing is training in building the foundations for all of these. Simply put, if our congregants don't trust us as leaders, it doesn't matter how skilled we are in all these other things. They. Will. Not. Follow. And conflict will ensue.

Building on the discussions from the coaching session, here are nine facets of leading change for us to keep in mind:

1. *Accentuate the Positive.* Many churches have grown accustomed to being criticized, abandoned, blown over, neglected, and chastised by pastors for not changing. They know they're declining. They know they're struggling. They know they're disappointing. It's easy for us as pastors to become disappointed with them for not meeting *our* expectations and to adopt a motto of "the criticism will continue till morale improves." Even if we don't criticize, our lack of giving them positive, loving messages will be interpreted as stony, silent criticism. Don't get caught up in disappointment. Instead, focus on showing compassion, understanding, and honoring pain from the past. Let them know you know how hard the change is and how great you think they are for trying anything.

2. *Slow the Pace.* Most pastors are in a hurry to make a mark for themselves in their careers. Just like people in the business world, they want to be seen as successful. Churches that resist us threaten our success. What percentage of mainline Protestant church pastors feel successful right now? We pastor in a culture that decreasingly cares about Christianity and church, in churches that struggle to grow. So, we become frustrated. In the face of frustration, we tend to speed up the pace of change and put more pressure on people because we're in a hurry to get on with it. *Slowing the pace reduces anxiety, nurtures trust, and allows details to more naturally emerge* (although it ironically increases pastoral anxiety because we're in a greater hurry for change to happen). Slowing down also helps them understand

us and what we are trying to do. So, when they resist, slow things down.

3. *Make the Steps Simpler*. Related to slowing the pace is simplifying the steps. Pastors are trained to understand complex ideas, and we're often able to hold onto many different ideas that intersect. We're able to do this because we generally have master-level training. Most laypeople has not had that level of training in regard to religion and the church. When the steps are complex, they become frustrated and opt out. So, for example, if we want to make the music of our worship service more up-to-date and relevant, we don't have to start with a praise band. We can emphasize playing more songs on the piano at a slightly faster tempo. Let that be the change for six months to a year. Then add more contemporary songs for another six months or a year. Then start talking about other instruments.

4. *Respect the Resistance*. Recognize that resistance is a legitimate response to past struggles and present stresses. Good therapists will always stop and let an anxious client know they understand the client's pain and ambivalence. They honor the client's pain and make it okay to feel afraid, even if acting out of fear isn't okay. When we let our church members know we understand how difficult change is and how hard it's been for them during their church's decline, it honors church leaders and their fears while simultaneously dispelling anxiety.

5. *Resist the Urge to Confront*. Confronting resistance increases resistance, especially early in ministry. Whether it's the secretly embedded confrontation in a sermon or calling members and leaders out for subverting you, direct confrontation often backfires. There are ways to work things out, but they must be built on a foundation of trust in and commitment to each other. An alternative to confrontation can take one of two forms, depending on the situation:

   A. *Convergence rather than confrontation*: Have a one-on-one or group conversation with others where you begin with a recognition of your shortfalls and frustrations. Start in a place of humility. Let the conversation naturally go to a place where each of you can share your thoughts and insights, and work through areas where you diverge. Then move to resolving the question "What do we do now?" But make sure the "what we do" is mutually agreed upon.

B. *Communal accountability:* We use the word "accountability" often in our modern culture, especially in the area of leadership. The problem is we tend to think of accountability as adequately following policies and procedures. Accountability is more than that. In a church, we are always accountable to God and the church community. This kind of accountability is more spiritual and relational. So, trying to enforce accountability on a one-on-one basis can often backfire because it turns personal. Dealing with accountability issues communally in a mutually supportive way often creates better outcomes. For instance, if the issue is one of professional problems with an employee or a volunteer of the church not following through with a responsibility, enlist the aid of other leaders in dealing with the situation. This can be a personnel committee, a pastoral relationship committee, or an ad hoc group. Have them create a circle of trust with you, the pastor, in order to identify the issue. Then have them create a course of action that is compassionate yet resolute, so the issue can be resolved in a way that brings people together instead of creating sides. This can include asking the difficult employee or church member to join in a process of working with the committee or group to offer feedback, insights, and input into the eventual decision. This way, the employee or church member becomes part of the process. The key is making this a communal approach, rather than a pastoral, one-on-one approach.

6. *Resist Being the Lone Expert.* We don't always have to be the expert-in-residence. Yes, church members don't have the education or training we do, but that doesn't mean they can't understand what we do. Instead of assuming they don't or won't get something, ensure they understand what you under-

stand. Help them develop expertise that allows them to be part-ners in change with you. Offer training and education. One of the approaches I've developed for transforming a church, which can be found in the last chapter of my book *Becoming a Blessed Church*, is the idea of creating *Transformational Task Forces.*[5] I gather a group of people to work together for three to fifteen months to develop an approach or a resolution for an issue, or to lead a transformation. A significant part of the process is educating people to the point where they understand the gist of what I understand, so we become experts together. They may resist the learning, but the process builds trust. The more resis-tant they are, the less expert we can be. The more trusting they are, the more expert we can be.

7. *Build on What They Can Do, Not on What They Can't.* Too often, pastors have their personal agendas and want certain things to happen. Thus, they push the church to develop the ministries and missions they want and get frustrated when the church acts apathetically. Wise pastors recognize that if the church mem-bers are older and lack energy for a certain program, they may still have the energy for other programs. They may not have the energy to revamp a children's education program, but they may have the energy for a prayer vigil, or a visitation ministry, or a dinner to raise money for mission. Help them build energy around what they can succeed at doing because that also builds trust in themselves and their abilities, which simultaneously builds confidence and energy for the future.

8. *Reframe Resistance in Positive Terms.* Be aware of how their resis-tance may actually be trying to preserve something cherished. Most members who resist us are also trying to preserve their community. Instead of criticizing them for not welcoming out-siders, find a way to praise them for their love of each other. Help them to feel good about what they do. Then challenge them to take that same love and turn it outward to visitors and new members. Invite them to become more welcoming by talking with them about how wonderfully welcoming they are with each other. Too often, pastors only see what's wrong with

members. They don't see that "what's wrong" may also be some things that are very right and can be the foundation for growth.

9. *Recognize Our Own Resistance.* Be aware that we also are resistant to changing our leadership style. We want them to change, but are we willing to change? Are we willing to slow ourselves down, to reduce or modify our ambitions, to change our style, to adapt ourselves to whatever may make us more trustworthy in their eyes? There are several methods for overcoming our resistances:

A. *Changing our leadership style:* If they aren't responding the way we want, perhaps we need to change them by changing ourselves. Are we being too cynical, too overbearing, too placating, too impatient, too indifferent, too aloof? Good pastoral leaders are constantly reading, listening, and learning how to become better leaders. They don't just confine their reading and learning to their comfort silos. As a moderate mainline Protestant church pastor, I read books and went to plenty of workshops by evangelical and even fundamentalist pastors. I also read books and went to workshops on organizational development (I'm including a bibliography of great secular and congregational organizational books at the end of this chapter). And I continued to go to trainings and read books on therapeutic techniques. These are some of the best places to learn how to be a pastor who engenders trust. The key is to discover wisdom from other silos as we break down our silos.

B. *Integrate other ideas:* Too often we cherish only ideas coming from our training and education. We become gatekeepers, squashing ideas from others and sowing seeds of distrust. Ideas that conflict with our cherished sacred cows—a Bible study from a rigid tradition, different kinds of music, or others—still may be good ideas for the church. At Calvin Presbyterian Church, we had groups that were not where I was theologically—Beth Moore studies, Dave Ramsey's Financial Peace University, and a very liberal fiction book group—but I recognized that these still brought people together, and my blessing on them nurtured trust. My foundation for saying yes was simply asking, "Do these help them grow in their relationship with God and each other?" If yes, I didn't stand in the way, even if I was uncomfortable with their theological stances.

C. *Detaching from our ideas*: Sometimes our ideas are right but won't work. There's nothing worse than forcing a fit that's not there. In the end, it frustrates us and sows distrust. Sometimes we just have to let go of our ideas to generate a greater community. So though we may be passionate about an idea, we may need to detach from it so it doesn't change our relationship with them, irrespective of whether the idea is accepted or not.

So, what are the steps you can take in reducing congregational resistance? The following exercise might help.

REDUCING RESISTANCE

A. Reflect on a past change that didn't go well in your church, examining it through the lens of what you've learned about the dynamics of resistance:

- *How did your church's anxiety lead them to resist?*
- *How might the attempted change have been too difficult for them, and how might we have tried too hard to change them?*
- *How was the proposed change not presented positively enough, and how did the consequences of staying the same not feel negative enough?*
- *How did we, as pastors, not create a positive enough interaction between leaders and members?*

B. Taking into account the insights from this chapter, outline in detail a different approach that might have reduced resistance and led to a better outcome.

Bibliography of Organizational Theory

Bolsinger, Tod. *Canoeing the Mountains: Christian Leadership in Uncharted Territory.* Downers Grove, IL: IVP Books, 2018.

Boyatzis, Richard E., and Annie McKee. *Resonant Leadership: Renewing Yourself and Connecting with Others through Mindfulness, Hope, and Compassion.* Boston: Harvard Business School Press, 2005.

Collins, Jim. *Good to Great: Why Some Companies Make the Leap . . . and Others Don't.* New York: HarperBusiness, 2001.

Heath, Chip, and Dan Heath. *Made to Stick: Why Some Ideas Survive and Others Die.* New York: Random House, 2007.

———. *Switch: How to Change Things When Change Is Hard.* New York: Broadway Books, 2010.

Pink, Daniel H. *Drive: The Surprising Truth about What Motivates Us.* New York: Riverhead Books, 2009.

———. *A Whole New Mind: Why Right-Brainers Will Rule the Future.* New York: Riverhead Books, 2005.

Sinek, Simon. *Start with Why: How Great Leaders Inspire Everyone to Take Action.* New York: The Penguin Group, 2009.

Tett, Gillian. *The Silo Effect: The Peril of Expertise and the Promise of Breaking Down Barriers.* New York: Simon & Schuster Paperbacks, 2015.

NOTES

1. N. Graham Standish, *In God's Presence: Encountering, Experiencing, and Embracing the Holy in Worship* (Lantham, MD: Rowman & Littlefield, 2010).

2. Chip Heath and Dan Heath, *Switch: How to Change Things When Change Is Hard* (New York: Broadway Books, 2010).

3. Adapted from Clifton W. Mitchell, *Effective Techniques for Dealing with Highly Resistant Clients*, 2nd ed. (Johnson City, TN: Clifton W. Mitchell Publishing, 2007), 1–47.

4. James Clear, *Atomic Habits: An Easy and Proven Way to Build Good Habits and Break Bad Ones* (New York: Avery, 2018).

5. N. Graham Standish, *Becoming a Blessed Church: Forming a Church of Spiritual Purpose, Presence, and Power* (Lanham, MD: Rowman & Littlefield, 2014), 167–91.

4

WRITING THE NEXT
FEW CHAPTERS

Sara is an Episcopal rector of a midsize, urban church. She's been its pastor for about four years and is struggling to figure out how to get the church to move forward. At several points in its history, this church had been larger and wealthier, but it has remained more traditional liturgically, even as it has embraced a more progressive theology.

She felt excitement at the beginning of her ministry there, but that's waned. Initially, the church's long history of being active in ministry and mission, along with an endowment to boost that activity, enthused her. Slowly, she realized while the endowment may be a blessing, it's also a curse. It keeps the church open, but it also staves off members' awareness that they need to do something to keep the church from slowly and inevitably dying. The members have become older, more tired, and even more stuck in a traditional way of doing everything—whether that means worship liturgy, the kinds of congregational activities in which they engage, and how they think about church in the face of changing times. The result is they talk about being active while actually being quite inactive. She feels church members have time for only each other and not for others, despite their proclaiming themselves mission-minded.

This was the third time we met. The previous two times we clarified her overall sense of disquiet over her ministry and her calling. In the previous session, we had ended with an assignment for her to reflect on her vision for the congregation she serves.

****

Graham: Sara, how are you doing today?

Sara: I don't know. I think I feel a little glum and maybe even a bit numb. Sorry for the rhyme. I also feel a bit irritated and a bit stuck. I've got a whole range of emotions forming tight little balls inside of me.

Graham: Which of those balls seems to rise the most?

Sara: (taking time to reflect) Probably "stuckness." I feel stuck, and all the other emotions come out of that.

Graham: Describe the "stuckness."

Sara: I just don't know where to take the church. It's like we have this ongoing cycle of sameness where they just keep doing what they've always done, and then I talk about perhaps doing new things, and then they go, "Yeah, yeah, we should do that," and then they don't do anything. There's no follow-up. There's no energy. They say yes, but it's more like they mean "maybe."

Graham: Well, that's clearer than where you were last time. You're starting to clarify things a bit.

Sara: Yeah. It helped to talk with you last time, but it also helped to talk with the bishop last week. I told her I was thinking of moving on. She told me that we can look into that but it would be hard to move me since I've been there for only four years. She's come in with a vision of crafting longer pastorates in our diocese. Of course, just when I'm thinking of making this a short pastorate! She's like, "Oh, Sara, I know you can do this. I believe in you. I think if you can stay for the long haul, you can turn them around." She's all positive, and I'm like, "What if I don't want to be there for the long haul?"

Graham: Is that you talking, or is that your disappointment and stuckness?

Sara: Good question. It's probably my knowing the bishop's right. And I don't want my bishop to be right. I want *me* to be right. Waaaaah! (smiles as she pretends to cry)

Graham: I've been there, making those same sounds.

Sara: Still, what do I do? They're the most pleasant do-nothings in the world. They're just content with where they are; but if they

84

keep going like this, they won't be where they are for too long. I don't know what to do. I can't get them to move beyond what they've done.

Graham: I can feel the stuckness in me as you're talking. I feel a bit stuck just listening to you. Like, I don't know what to say. I'm a bit stuck in your stuckness.

Sara: Well, that's great! Now we're both stuck! Sorry to be like my church.

Graham: Doesn't mean I *am* stuck, and it doesn't mean that *you're* actually stuck. We both just *feel* stuck. Feeling and being aren't the same.

Sara: They feel the same.

Graham: They do! And it's a powerful feeling because feelings of stuckness paralyze our brains. They drain us, making it hard to think creatively.

Sara: Yeah, and I'm a bit drained.

Graham: Do you know what you remind me of? You remind me of an author who has writer's block. You know you have a story inside you. You've told part of the story. But you're stuck on chapter 6 and you don't know what to do next. It feels like the characters have backed you into a literary corner, and you don't know how to write your way out of it. You've lost creativity because you're stuck in a silent battle with the characters of your story, the church's story. You want to write chapter 7, but they're saying to you, "No, no, no! Take us back to chapter 4. We liked it there. We don't want this story to go any further." You want to go forward, but they're telling you they want to keep repeating the same two or three chapters indefinitely.

Sara: Yeah, that's it. When I first started there, I felt like I had a lot of creativity. That lasted about two years. The story was exciting. We had all sorts of possible futures. Then we started settling in. They got over the initial excitement about me. And I got over my initial excitement about them. Since then, we've settled into boring. And no one's going to buy this novel because it's boring. That's why we don't get many visitors returning.

Graham: You know, I like this metaphor of us being authors and our churches being like the characters of a story we write. It gives insight into things we wouldn't normally notice. Not only are you an author and they're the characters and context, but it's like this story is a multi-author story.

Sara: What do you mean?

Graham: You're not the only author. This story has been going on since—when was your church founded?

Sara: I think it was 1893.

Graham: Okay, so this story began 132 years ago—

Sara: Um, 126 years ago.

Graham: Yeah, I suck at math. Anyway, your story began 126 years ago. And it's had a number of pastors, probably somewhere around ten to fifteen.

Sara: Probably.

Graham: And each pastor is responsible for about one, two, or three chapters, depending on how long they've stayed there and what they managed to lead the congregation through. Some pastors just maintain what's been, so their time there is like a long, slow chapter. Others, like me, were clearly writing numerous chapters while leading churches through several different capital campaigns, renovations, constructions, but also through the development of new ministries and missions that necessitated the campaigns.

The onset of each pastor's leadership represents the beginning of a new chapter, since leaders always represent new directions and adaptations for a church. Interim periods are simply meant to be times of finishing up a previous chapter so a new one can begin. As a result, they almost act like summaries and transitions. So, you were given the story at about chapter 28 or so. You didn't get to read many of the previous chapters, just summaries. You were simply told, "Here's the story. Now write the next bunch of chapters. Oh, and we're not going to make it easy." You've been trying to do that, but you don't know the characters, history, or context well enough. You've just been told to write. How can you *not* get writer's block?

Sara: I guess we should call it pastor's block.

Graham: We should. I'll add a bit more now that I'm on a roll. You've also been trained in seminary and elsewhere that there's a standard set of chapters you have to write. So, if you're evangelical, you're supposed to write chapters on going out and making disciples. If you're more progressive, it's to go out and be more missional. And if you're Episcopalian . . .

Sara: It's to make people like liturgy and sacraments again, while also going out and standing up for the oppressed and the marginalized.

Graham: The problem is you're grafting other people's visions for what the church's next chapters should be onto your congregation. That's not bad, but it's a reason I had you do the visioning exercise last week. I wanted to get to what *your* vision for the church is, not just the denomination's, the seminary's, or some book's. I wanted to hear your authentic dream for what the congregation can become. I wanted to hear about what chapters you're called to write, not the chapters your professors and denomination want you to write. They're not leading your church, and many of them have simply given you an updated, 1970s script for the church they cherished and want you to lead your church back to.

Sara: I'm seeing what you're saying. I did the exercise. Do you want to go over it?

Graham: I do, but let's wait a bit. I want to explore this writer's-block idea with you more and then come back to your vision. I want to see if writer's block is a good metaphor for what you're struggling with.

Sara: Pastor's block!

Graham: Right, right! I read a fascinating book years ago called *Story* by Robert McKee.[1] McKee is considered the guru for scriptwriters, screenwriters, and novelists. His students have earned many, many Academy and Emmy nominations and awards. Reading his book, I realized the principles of screenwriting are similar to the principles of pastoring. We're all telling a story. The difference is you're leading a congregation to live out that story. It's not in your head the way a story is. It's your life.

Sara: That's interesting. There are times when I feel like I'm trying to write a story, but the characters aren't cooperating.

Graham: Yeah, that's the pastor's block.

Sara: How do I get them to cooperate?

Graham: By realizing the block is in you, not them. You want them to become something they aren't or aren't ready to be. In the face of this gap between what you want and who they are, they and you get paralyzed by indecision and confusion.

Sara: I'm certainly paralyzed by that.

Graham: (grabs McKee's book from a bookshelf) If you can indulge me a bit more, let me read to you what McKee says about writer's block. He believes writer's block arises from bad writing, where authors are blocked by their unwillingness to let the story unfold and instead they try to force it to fit their obsessions. Give me a second to find the quote ... Here it is:

> When talented people write badly, it's generally for one of two reasons: Either they're blinded by an idea they feel compelled to prove or they're driven by an emotion they must express. When talented people write well, it is generally for this reason: They're moved by a desire to touch the audience.[2]

Here's the book. Read the quote again to yourself.

Sara: (after reading) Okay, so how does this translate to ministry?

Graham: While you were reading, I printed out a version of this I adapted to ministry when I first read the book. Here's what it says:

> When talented pastors lead badly, it's generally for one of two reasons: Either they're blinded by a *theological ideal* they feel compelled to prove or they're driven by a *personal agenda* they must accomplish. When talented pastors lead well, it is generally for this reason: They're moved by a desire to *spiritually and compassionately* touch their members.

Sara: I think I'm catching this, but say more.

Graham: Read it again and ask yourself a question: "Is there a theological ideal you're trying constantly to prove or a personal agenda you're trying constantly to accomplish?" If so, how can you focus more on spiritually and compassionately touching members?

Sara: Wow! Yes, if I'm being honest with myself. My agenda is for them to do more and grow. I want the church to be more active so I can point to it and say I'm the pastor of an active church. I suppose I do have a theological ideal, which is social justice, but I just want them to be active and grow. I keep thinking if I just do *this* or *that*, they'll grow.

Graham: And then you'll be successful.

Sara: Yes, then I'll be successful.

Graham: The problem is the more you push, the less they do.

Sara: Yes!

Graham: It's like what we in the marital counseling business call the pursuer-distancer effect. The more you pursue someone, the more they distance from you. It's like walking into a bar hoping to meet the person of your dreams. You never do. But when you're not looking, that's when it happens.

Sara: And I've been pursuing them. I've kind of been pushing them. Are they distancing from me?

Graham: Well, you get pretty frustrated when they don't do more, right? And that causes you to push them harder to do more, right? And they're doing less, right?

Sara: Yes! I hadn't thought about it like being in a bar, but I'm definitely the pastor who's walking in and looking for someone to do something. Gawd, I hope I don't come across as desperate like one of those straw-sippers.

Graham: Straw-sippers?

Sara: You know, those women who sit there sipping their cocktails, looking around for someone to notice them.

Graham: Yeah, I don't see you as a straw-sipper. You're too confident for that. But you're getting the point. Going back to the earlier metaphor, you've got pastor's block because you've been desperately trying to push an agenda. But writer's—or pastor's—block also comes when you have too many ideas and you don't know where to go because you haven't spent enough time grounding your vision in their context.

Sara: What do you mean by that?

Graham: Just like writing a novel, you have a setting, a context, and a cast of characters. Good authors don't have a vision for a romance set at a beachside resort with people on vacation and then suddenly turn it into a thriller set in a monastery. You have to stick with a solid vision and its context.

I had you write a vision statement, which we'll get to before we're done. Your vision has to be set in a definite context and situation. So before looking at your story's vision, let's look at its context.

Sara: Wait, your "story's vision"? I was thinking story and vision were the same.

Graham: Sorry about that. Vision is the basic plot rumbling around in your head that you want to become the story. Story is how that plot gets played out in that particular context, with those particular characters, in that particular time and space.

Sara: Okay. So, vision is plot that gets turned into story.

Graham: Yes. So, let's look at your church's context. Tell me about your church—how it started, how it's been, what its context and all is.

Sara: Well, it's not like I've studied its history a whole lot, but I'll try.

Graham: Yeah, I'm not looking for a David McCullough history. Just what you know.

Sara: David McCullough?

Graham: Never mind! (laughs) Showing my age. Just give me the context.

Sara: It's in an urban area now; but when the church started, it was in a suburb of the city. It was the hilly, shady area where people built nice homes away from the pollution and poverty. I think the homes overlooked the factories the owners had established below, in the distance and across the river. A lot of the original residents were rich, white people of English and Scottish descent. They were the elite. They were Episcopalian. What can I say?

But from what I've heard and read, they cared about the workers and the people who didn't have much. I think they did a lot of mission stuff to try to make the lives of the workers better, even though the workers were Catholic. I'm guessing it was the women who did most of this ministry with the workers, which makes sense today because the women tend to be more active now than the men.

Graham: So, would you say this has been an active, women-driven church?

Sara: I hadn't thought of it that way, but yeah.

Graham: It's interesting they've called a woman pastor.

Sara: Yep, and that's a bit different for them. I'm wondering if they've always been a women's church but felt like they needed a supportive man leading them.

Graham: That's *really* good insight. Hold onto that. So, what's its more recent history?

Sara: I think it's been in decline like most Episcopal churches over the past twenty years. They talk a lot about how the church used to be, and in my interviews with them, they talked about hoping to recapture what they had. Their wanting to recapture the past felt very hopeful when I first came to the church because it seemed like a strong desire to move forward, but now it feels like they're tired and content to reminisce about the past.

Graham: That may be the case, but that may not be what they want to do.

Sara: What do they want to do?

Graham: That's where you come in. You're the author. But remember what I said before. You can't just change the characters, the context, and the previous plot. Think about what the plot of this church has been. It's had a story it's told. What's that story been?

Sara: Okay. A church of women helping people now in decline.

Graham: Really? (laughs) That's the best you can do? You're. The. Author. Give me a plot.

Sara: Okay. I think I'd say it was a church started by successful, English/Scottish families who cared about progress, cared about industry, and cared about people. It was very successful for a long time. Then the world changed around them. They weren't as wealthy, the factories closed, and since then they've been lost.

Graham: There you go. That's very good. So, what kinds of chapters can you write starting from there? What vision do you bring that changes the plot and thereby changes the story?

Sara: That's a good question . . . I'm not sure. I don't want to create some fantasy where I "rescue" the church and become a hero.

Graham: Yeah, I don't think this is a hero story. I think it's more like a "slice-of-life" story that speaks to how they live and transform. It's a story grounded in their reality. Let me share some other insights from that McKee book. He has some really good ones that may translate. One is this quote that I love, but that's also hard to translate into ministry: "Story isn't a flight from reality but a vehicle that carries us on our search for reality, our best effort to make sense out of the anarchy of existence."[3] What do you make of this quote?

Sara: Um . . . "Story isn't a flight from reality but . . ." How did the rest go?

Graham: "But a vehicle that carries us on our search for reality." It makes sense of the anarchy of existence.

Sara: Wow! So my ministry isn't meant to be a flight from reality but an attempt to help people make sense of life.

Graham: Yes! So what does that mean for you?

Sara: I'm going to have to think about this for a while, but I think it means I keep trying to create this "perfect" church, which might be a fantasy. What I'm truly supposed to do is to help them figure out how to live.

Graham: Those are your next chapters: *How do they live in the reality in which they are, but in a new way?* And how do you help them get there? He had another quote that's related: "Flawed and false storytelling is forced to substitute spectacle for substance, trickery for truth. Weak stories, desperate to hold audience attention, degenerate into multimillion-dollar razzle-dazzle demo reels."[4]

Sara: Don't make me think too hard about this. My head's already pretty full. What does that mean to you, and how does it relate to me? It sounds profound.

Graham: I think it means many churches out there that have lost their plot and struggle with pastor's block resort to razzle-dazzle. For example, many churches try to offer contemporary worship. This isn't a critique of contemporary churches, because many of them are doing it authentically. It's a genuine part of *their* next few chapters. Still, most churches are trying to figure out how to get more people to join their church, and so they resort to flash and dash, gimmicks and mimics. You have to be authentically who you are as a church of

92

substance. You're Episcopalian. You are part of a deep, sacramental tradition with a concern for others who may not be like you. How do you dip into that tradition and make it part of the next few chapters, plunging into the unknown?

Sara: Hmmm, it's like not trying to follow the trends but start with who the church authentically is, and then build from there. So, what do I do?

Graham: I'm not the author. You are. You have to grapple with this. I can give you pointers, but you have to be the one to lead them. Still, I can give you several hints.

First, *their story is your story.* You can't take them where you aren't willing to go. Whatever it is you want them to do, you can't lead them there from the rear. You have to lead them by walking ahead of them and making the pathway forward feel safe for them. I know that for me, in my church, I wanted them to be a deeply spiritual church that bravely followed God's call for them. To do that, I had to constantly work on my anxieties and fears that I wouldn't be able to hear God, or God would abandon me and everything would fail. Then I had to use what I learned through my struggles to help them overcome their fears. And I had to start out slowly. I couldn't ask them to join me where I was at the time. I had to ask them to join me where I was years before and then think out the steps to move forward to where I was at that point.

So I spent a lot of time trying to figure out how to make the trail easier for them than it was for me. I also had to be sensitive to their resistance, reluctance, anxieties, and fears. When they pulled back, I had to pull back too.

I'll give you the second one in a moment. What are your thoughts about this first one?

Sara: I hadn't thought about it this way. In other words, I can be involved in the ministries I'm passionate about, whether or not they have a passion for it, and then lead out of what I've learned by pursuing my passion.

Graham: Yes, lead out of what you're passionate about, and only lead out of what other people are passionate about where those things intersect with yours. I've been a pastor long enough to see so many trends go by—the pastoral care movement, the discipleship movement, the purpose-driven movement, the spirituality movement (of which I was a part), the missional movement, the adaptive leadership movement. They're all absolutely right. And they're all incredibly helpful. And they all fall short at some level because they can inhibit pastors from doing what they have a passion for. Movements like these are inherently saying, "No, no, no, *this* is what you need to do!" We don't have to ignore them, but we need to use them to help us learn how to pursue our callings and passions. So, what is your passion?

Sara: Ugh! I have to figure out what my passion is?

Graham: That was part of the vision exercise we did over the past week. Again, we have another thirty minutes, so let's get to that in a few minutes. I'll share a second hint first.

Sara: Okay.

Graham: Second, *your story needs surprise.* All stories need surprise. That's why we love mysteries so much, and why the prime-time slots on television are filled with police, legal, and hospital dramas. They allow for major surprises every ten minutes as you find out the person you thought was guilty couldn't be guilty because he was having an affair with the head of nursing *and* the head of the legal department at the same time. You know what I mean?

Sara: Um, sort of. I tend to scroll through YouTube videos in the evening.

Graham: Even better. Each video is a surprise, especially as you keep clicking on new videos that show up on the right side of the screen.

Sara: Got it. Surprise them.

Graham: Don't want to bore you, but here's what McKee says: "We go to the storyteller with a prayer: 'Please, let it be good. Let it give me an experience I've never had, insights into a fresh truth. Let me laugh at something I've never thought funny. Let me be moved by something that's never touched me before. Let me see the world in a new way. Amen.' In other words, the audience prays for surprise, the reversal of expectations."[5]

Sara: So, how do I surprise them?

Graham: By taking whatever your passion is and sharing it with them in new ways. For me, it came in a lot of ways. Remember, my passion was helping the congregation become spiritually deep. So, when we integrated video projections into our worship, it wasn't so we could project contemporary hymns; it was so I could surprise them as I taught.

For example, when teaching them about being open to God's presence already in their midst but that they can't see, I showed a film clip from *Field of Dreams*. Do you know that film?

Sara: Yep!

Graham: You know the part where the kid chokes on the hot dog while the brother-in-law yells at Ray to sell the farm because he's going broke, and he can't see the baseball players in the background playing ball because they're sort of ghosts or something like that?[6]

Sara: Yeah.

Graham: As the girl chokes, a 1920s rookie baseball player, Moonlight Graham, comes off the field, transforms into his 1970s-older-doctor self, and dislodges the hot dog from the choking girl. Suddenly the brother-in-law sees the ballplayers and says, "Where did they come from?" Realizing Ray was right all along, he says, "Ray, don't sell the farm!" I used that as a surprising film clip to talk about how we often have to believe God is there before we can see God there.

I also used PowerPoint to show pictures. For example, I did one sermon on experiencing Christ, and I showed about thirty different artistic representations that had been created over the years. One was of a crucifix with Jesus in a gymnast jumpsuit, head slumped, while holding his arms straight out holding onto still rings.[7] I used that to teach people we all have our cherished images of Christ that can get in the way of experiencing Christ, but it's when we let them go that we begin to truly experience Christ in our lives.

I surprised them in other ways. I did a sermon where I wanted to tell a story about an experience our associate pastor had, so I had her come up and tell it during my sermon. Then I came back up and reflected on it.

Other times, we had members create five-minute Advent videos on the Advent theme for that Sunday. We played the videos before lighting the Advent wreath. These were some of the most amazing videos ever, ranging from dance to comedies to stop-action Lego videos.

We also had guests come and talk to our members and the community about interesting topics during the week. We had one who spoke about Christian faith and healing. Another was a pastor who was a professional-grade photographer. He showed his nature photos. Another spoke about alternative ways of being healthy.

We did small groups based on topics such as science and spirituality, near-death experiences, women's issues, and contemplative prayer, that deepened their experiences of God, but that were also somewhat surprising. The key was always keeping one foot rooted in the vision, and the other in possibility.

The struggle is when we are pastors of traditional churches, we worry people will want only what they've already had, and we'll be criticized for trying something new. And the truth is we will be criticized. But movies are criticized too. There's a whole industry devoted to criticizing them. But people keep making them, and people keep watching them.

Sara: I'm starting to think about surprising things I could be doing. This is kind of energizing.

Graham: Cool! I'm going to add a last insight into this. If you are going to embark on this, *you have to be both patient and persevering.* Don't do all of this on one Sunday. Think about where you want them to go, think about surprising ways to move them there, but don't rush. You have several chapters to write. Let them unfold. No good author packs a chapter with three chapters' worth of action.

So, let's get to your vision. What did you come up with?

Sara: Okay, let me pull it up on my phone. Last week we talked about me liking the fact we're sacramental and how much I value that. I also talked about how I want this church to go out and care about people. So, I came up with this: "Rooted in sacraments while sharing the gospel."

Graham: Good. That's a very good start. Now, you're going to hate me for this next part: get rid of the religious jargon. Keep "sacramental," but get rid of "sharing the gospel."

Sara: Why?

Graham: Because you're going to use this to clearly communicate to others what your vision is so you can then insert it into the congregation's story. "Sharing the gospel" is code. It's used so much that it becomes meaningless when we're trying to communicate something deeper to people who don't always get Christian code.

Sara: So, what do I change it to?

Graham: Well, what does it mean to you?

Sara: Uh . . . I don't know.

Graham: See, that's why we're going to get rid of it. If you can't explain it, they're not necessarily going to understand it. Let's break your vision down. Hold onto the sacramental part because it's very much part of your vision and your church's history. What are you *really* hoping to do now that you're rooted in sacrament?

Sara: I'm trying to get people to see the world as Jesus saw it and sees it now. I want them to realize everything is holy. Everything is full of God's presence. I want people to see beauty and hope and possibility.

Graham: *Great!* That's very good! So how do you put that in there instead of "sharing the gospel"?

Sara: How about this: "Rooted in sacraments, seeing life as a sacrament."

Graham: That's very good. Can I offer a tweak? You don't have to go with it, but it may make it a little clearer to someone new to your church who isn't used to religious language.

Sara: Yeah.

Graham: How about, "Rooted in sacrament, living life as sacred"? Or something like that.

Sara: I like that. It says I'm rooted in the sacraments that give me life and I'm also trying to live a life where I experience the sacred in everything and everyone.

Graham: Yeah, that's what I'm sensing. Now here's the challenge. How do you write that vision, that basic plot, into the next few chapters of your church's story, while being faithful to the characters, context, and history of your church? You're trying to lead a sacramental church to see and act in life as sacred. How do you lead them in that direction?

Sara: Yeah, that's the challenge, but I'm feeling like I have something of a vision now. I'm kind of energized. I feel like I'm starting to get ideas too. Like maybe once a week I could take some of the members of the church on a "sacred walk" where we just walk in different parts of our neighborhood and pray for the neighborhoods and the people there as we do. We can begin with a prayer and come back to the church and have a short eucharistic liturgy at the end.

Graham: That's so cool! I like it.

Sara: Thanks. It really helps because it feels like it takes the pressure off. I don't have to do all these things to grow the church. I can actually have fun while letting the sacred stuff bubble up.

Graham: Yes! Okay, let's stop here so you can take a sacred drive home as you come up with lots of sacred ideas.

Sara: Cool!

FURTHER THOUGHTS

Reading *Story* by Robert McKee helped me to look at church as an ongoing narrative unfolding the history of my ministry.[8] We don't know how it will end. All we know is as pastoral leaders, our role is to be like authors working in conjunction with the characters we already have as we craft an engaging story. Too often we try to recreate our churches using another church's story. We try to imitate other, seemingly more successful churches. Or we try to recreate the vision a professor or a favorite religious writer had for what church ideally should be. In all these cases, we treat the church as though we are working with a cast of characters different from the folks who are actually there. But we're not called to be those pastors leading their real or mythological churches. We're called to be authentic authors who have been given the authority to help write the next few chapters of *our* congregation's ongoing story. We hope our legacy will live on and influence future chapters, but we have no control over that.

The question is, will we be creative authors who allow the story to unfold? Or will we be authors with writer's block because we're pushing an agenda rooted in our own unmet needs or pursuing an unrealistic theological ideal? Or will we write new chapters more appropriate for a different set of characters and context? To be good authors of our congregation's next few chapters, here are some pointers that may help clarify the process of nurturing the church's story:

- *Good stories are composed of a series of smaller stories.* Can we see the ministries and missions of our churches as the smaller stories that make up the larger one? Can we see each Sunday of worship as a smaller story that makes up the larger one? It's in these smaller stories that transformation takes place. As we put together worship, education, program, pastoral care, and mission activities, how do we make sure they remain authentically rooted in our larger pastoral vision while being compatible with and congenial to the congregation's context? Each of those smaller events is a story in and of itself. Can we construct them in an ongoing, larger narrative where we hope that people will be *just a little bit different* after each one?
- *The smaller stories are always about transformation.* This wasn't reflected as much in the coaching dialogue above, but stories are also always about transformation. Congregations are always about transformation—transforming members, the church itself, the community, the culture, and ourselves. This transformation may be positive or negative, but it's always taking place, even in churches that are trying to stay the same. It's just that, in the latter, the transformation becomes more negative over time.

What causes us to struggle is that whenever we or anyone else undergoes transformation, it always ushers in discomfort and a small measure of discontinuity. Most people want change (no matter how much they protest), but they're always uncomfortable as they wander through it, which is why they start to resist it. Most conflict doesn't arise at the beginning or end of change. It arises in the middle, as they grieve the loss of what was while struggling with doubts because of their impatience to get to where they are going. Like the

Israelites in Exodus, they do know they can't go back, but they're not ready to see what may be. Pastors have to be authors who gently but firmly move their congregations through these transformations. Stories with no transformation are boring. Churches with no transformation are boring.

- *Transformations are always surprising.* People like surprise as long as the surprises are positive or have the potential to be. We discussed this above. Just remember it's the hopeful surprises that keep people moving forward. Can even painful surprises be reframed to be understood as the birth pangs of much better surprises?
- *Smaller stories build into major transformations.* As said above, each program and activity of the church is a story on its own. With good leadership, each activity, event, ministry, and mission has a purpose. That purpose serves the larger vision. As pastors and authors of that larger story, we're responsible for ensuring this collection of smaller stories leads to the larger story we're trying to tell in our congregations.

So if we're to help a church write new chapters, how do you do that? The following guidelines may help:

- *Start with where the church is,* rather than where you wish it to be.
- *Take time to understand the church's characters, context, and conditions.* Get to know your church's history. Get a clear sense of who the characters are, especially the prominent ones. Listen to your congregation's stories by caring about them as they talk about the church in individual and group conversations: *How did they start? When were they vibrant? When and how did they experience God? What happened that changed things? Why are they still with the church?* These conversations can be planned, but often they are spontaneous, arising unexpectedly through the natural interactions of the congregation.
- *Slowly introduce a new narrative that's congruent with their history.* Understand your leadership vision for the church and find ways to begin talking about it in a language members can

100

understand and support. Craft a congregational narrative that helps you intuitively understand who and why they are so you can then understand how you can move them to where you're leading them.

- *Progressively but evenly gain momentum and begin introducing transformative surprises* that engage people with your vision.
- You and they will eventually reach a point where everyone is no longer in familiar territory, but *everyone will want to see how it all unfolds.*

The following exercise may help you to craft your vision and then figure out how to articulate it into the life of your church:

FINDING YOUR PURPOSE

Every pastor has a grounding purpose. There's a reason you were called into ministry and to your church. Following that purpose in a healthy way allows your ministry to become healthy. That purpose, that why, is still part of who you are and why you are in ministry.

Unfortunately, we can become confused about or forget what our original purpose and calling are. We get overwhelmed by the complexity of ministry, as well as the uncertainty of it. When that happens, we may fall prey either to focusing on doing what makes people complain less or on imitating what other pastors are doing, thus moving further away from our original purpose.

The following exercise is designed to help you to understand more clearly what your purpose is so you can listen better for how God is calling you to adapt to a changing culture around you.

Reflect on what you felt and experienced that led you to explore ministry.

- *What "golden experience" or "meaningful event" led you to consider that God might be calling you to ministry?*
- *Reflect on why you think God called you into pastoral ministry. As you do, list those qualities, aspects, and skills you have that you believe God wanted you to use in your leadership and ministry.*

Reflect on your answers to the previous questions and try to finish the following sentences (they can be long):

- *Reflecting on my experiences in life, I have felt the greatest sense of meaning and purpose when I _____.*

- *In my ministry, the thing that has given me the greatest sense of meaning and purpose is helping people to _____.*

Reflecting on your previous sentences, try to complete the following:

- *My purpose is to _____, which I live out when I _____.*

Take this previous sentence and turn it into a simple, personal vision statement:

- *My purpose in ministry is to _____.*

Refine this sentence by removing vague religious language such as "spread the gospel" or "incarnate Christ in the community." Put it into concrete language that could be used to communicate your vision to someone who does not know Christian language.

The final sentence is now a statement you can use as a guide to become the author of the church's next few chapters in its present context and climate, and as it faces new challenges.

102

NOTES

1. Robert McKee, *Story: Substance, Structure, Style, and the Principles of Screen-writing* (New York: ReganBooks, 1997).

2. McKee, *Story*, 7.

3. McKee, *Story*, 12.

4. McKee, *Story*, 13.

5. McKee, *Story*, 355.

6. *Field of Dreams*, directed by Phil Alden Robinson (1989; Universal City, CA: Universal Studios Home Entertainment, 2011), Blu-ray.

7. "Jesus the Gynmast," image taken by Timo Kauppi, October 28, 2011, https://tinyurl.com/stjv84v. Also see image taken by kh1234567890 on August 17, 2005, https://tinyurl.com/v9vtwrn.

8. For a more detailed perspective on this, please see N. Graham Standish, "Pastor as Narrative Leader," in *Living Our Story: Narrative Leadership and Congregational Culture*, ed. Larry A. Golemon (Lanham, MD: Rowman & Littlefield, 2010), 63–88.

5

CAN WE CHANGE THE SYSTEM?

Joshua is the senior pastor of a midsize, multistaffed Disciples of Christ church. He has been at the church for almost two years. Before his arrival, the church had struggled financially and relationally through two dysfunctional pastorates over the course of ten years. It shrunk from about 800 members to 250, and from 300 average attendance to 125.

Joshua spent the first year trying to get a comprehensive sense of the church. Having read a lot of the works by Edwin Friedman and Peter Steinke on family systems theory and its application to understanding church systems, he's been focused on trying to change the church's system and lead it out of its ongoing dysfunction. He knows he needs to change the system of the church, but he's afraid of creating conflict along the way that will resurrect the dysfunctions of the past. This is our second meeting.

****

Graham: So, you made it?

Joshua: I did! I wasn't sure I'd be able to get through all the construction in time to get here, but I'm only five minutes late, which surprises me.

Graham: Not a problem. It helped me to finish up something. So how are things going since the last time we met?

Joshua: Good question. I left here with a lot to think about regarding the nature of dysfunction. The thing that really got me was your saying dysfunction doesn't mean "not functioning," but instead "functioning in pain." That helped because I had been thinking of it simply as not getting things done, so my focus was on how to get them to start getting things done. The realization that dysfunction means functioning in pain helped me understand how some of the ways I was going to implement change would have created pain because they would have had me criticizing them. Your comment saying you can't criticize people out of dysfunction makes sense.

Graham: Good. I've seen a lot of pastors try to criticize churches to better health. It's a weird approach. I used to have a funny poster in our church office that said, "The beatings will continue until morale improves." I think the pastoral equivalent might be, "The criticisms will continue until you become more motivated!"

Joshua: Right, and my frustrations were getting to the point where I wanted to motivate them through criticism. It wasn't going to be harsh, but it was going to be slightly critical in a way that was going to try to get them to own up to their past dysfunction. The phrase I kept using was "hold them accountable." I realize now I was about to stick my toe into dysfunctional waters and perhaps start making the same mistakes my predecessors did. I was going to hold them accountable for relationships of the past where dysfunction was sparked by inadequate pastoral leadership.

Graham: In other words, you were going to hold them responsible for previous pastors leading in dysfunctional ways. What do you know about them?

Joshua: The pastors? Not a whole lot other than one was truly disliked and the other wasn't very respected. From what they've told me, Clyde—the pastor previous to the pastor before me—was kind of an odd person. He was very intellectual and would say, "My role isn't to be your friend. My role is to teach you God's word."

Graham: Yikes! I'll bet that went over well.

Joshua: It may be what they *thought* they wanted in a pastor at the time. I was told they wanted someone who was more intellectual because the pastor before him, who was beloved, wasn't a good preacher. So, they got his opposite—a guy who was disliked by most and despised by some, but who could give very erudite sermons that bored them over time. Apparently, he didn't have much time for relationships. His whole thing was theology and Bible. Relationships didn't matter. Only theology and rightness did.

Graham: What about the one you followed?

Joshua: Cindy? I think she was Clyde's opposite. According to what I've heard, she was nice but not a very good leader. She liked to visit people and they liked her sermons, but she was very disorganized. The dysfunction around her was similar to and different from Clyde's. His dysfunction came out of his being arrogant and dismissing people. It resulted in a group of people in the church banding together to push him out.

With Cindy, I think the issue was she created a vacuum that members of the church stepped into, many of whom were the people who pushed Clyde out. The fact Cindy was incredibly nice and didn't want to offend anyone made it easy for those who were offensive to step up and try to recreate the church in their own image.

I've been very careful to be friends with these people and to seek their advice at times, even when I didn't need it. I recognize they're now experienced in making things uncomfortable for pastors.

Graham: That's brilliant! You don't know how often I've talked with pastors about seeking the guidance of those who pose a danger to them. Too many pastors see these members as subversive enemies in a power struggle and then try to grapple for power with them. When you have a group that's been successful at grasping power in the past, they're more experienced than any incoming pastor at using their power. The pastor almost always loses.

So, what led Cindy to leave?

Joshua: I think they made her miserable. She kept trying harder and harder to be nice to them, and they became meaner and meaner. In her mind, she was responding to hate with love. I think in their minds, she wasn't doing her job.

Graham: Is this what church people have told you?

Joshua: Actually, it's what she told me. I met with her about three months after I came to the church, and we talked for two hours. I think I was more a counselor for her after a while. She had a lot to get off her chest. She's not in ministry right now. Her experience left a bitter taste in her mouth. She's now working as a personal trainer. I have to say I was jealous of her when we met because she's in much better shape than me.

Graham: Than all of us, I imagine. It's hard to be nice and be a good leader. That doesn't mean you can't be nice as a leader, but you have to lead first while simultaneously finding a way to be gracious in leading. If you just want to be liked, it's hard to lead. You have to balance gentleness with firmness, which is very hard to do.

Joshua: I think she was undone by her gentleness. At any rate, in both cases, her wanting to be liked created the conditions for a small group to form among the members and sow dysfunction, and they're still there. Like I said, I've tried to make friends with them and have periodically sought them out for advice I didn't need.

Graham: So, where'd you get the idea for that?

Joshua: It's something I read in Edwin Friedman's book *Generation to Generation.*[1] Do you know this book?

Graham: I do. Actually, I'm pretty well versed in the whole systems approach Friedman, Peter Steinke, and others teach. Before feeling called to be a pastor, I first felt called to be a marital and family therapist, which is why I got a Master of Social Work. The program I studied in was steeped in systems theory. I read *Generation to Generation* in 1987 as part of my social work internship as a pastoral counselor. It was wonderful in extending my thinking of systems theory into all of life. As a result, I tend to think intuitively in terms of systems theory because I was simultaneously studying family systems writers like Salvador Minuchin, Virginia Satir, and Murray Bowen.

Anyway, what did Friedman say?

Joshua: He said something that's stuck with me; it's to the effect of, "If a leader is clear about his or her leadership and is willing to continually listen to others and share his or her ideas, the church will generally go along."[2]

Graham: That's it! And as you've seen, that especially includes those who could undermine what you do. It's like marital therapy: don't take one person's side but keep connected to both, regardless of how you feel about one person or the other. Listen deeply and offer clear guidance in response.

Joshua: Yeah, and that's what I try to do.

Graham: How has that left you feeling about the next steps in your leadership?

Joshua: I'm both excited and scared. I want to start pushing them more, but I'm afraid of messing things up because of my predecessors' experiences. I don't want to end up like them.

Graham: Not sure you will. You don't come across to me as the "arrogant preacher" or the "wanting to be liked" sort.

Joshua: I know, but at the same time I'm very aware that over the years, the church has created a lot of triangles I have to detangle.

Graham: Give me an example.

Joshua: Well, there's one that existed between the music director and the previous pastors, which has persisted throughout the interim periods. There's always been conflict there. I think he's building conflict with me, too, but I'm trying to avoid stepping into the triangle.

Graham: How?

Joshua: I don't know. I'm not quite sure. It feels like there's budding conflict between us, but I can't tell if there is or if that's just my paranoia.

Graham: Tell me what's going on.

Joshua: It's about who picks hymns. According to my denomination, I'm the one who gets to pick them. But the music director insists on picking them, and the hymns he picks are almost always complex classical ones. I want to pick more singable ones. I'm not a great fan of contemporary Christian music, but I recognize more and more members of the congregation listen to it on Christian music stations, and they want more of that.

Graham: So how do you detriangulate there?

Joshua: It's confusing because I'm not sure what the triangle is.

Graham: I'm guessing you're struggling with an *authority triangle*. When there's conflict between you two, and it feels as if there's no way to resolve it directly, the triangle forms. In this case, it's over who has the *authority* to choose music, which is the third point of the triangle. Any time there's an authority issue that isn't resolved directly, you get a dysfunctional triangle that makes it painful to deal with one another. What makes it worse is now that there's an issue over who has authority, it's easy to rope others into the triangle. Your music director will get the choir to form a sub-triangle—a coalition—where they agree with him that he has the authority. And now the triangle becomes more dysfunctional because you have to find and form a coalition with people to give you more power. The problem is that the ones who seem to have a more vested interest in waging this battle are those who deal with the music every week—the musicians and the choir. The more you both search for people to back each of your sides, the more dysfunctional the triangle becomes because no one's talking directly. They're all looking for political advantage.

Unfortunately, the issue is who's the worship *music* authority; and when there's conflict over this, your music director generally wins because it rationally seems like it's his job, and because he's won these conflicts in the past. He's the one who *knows* music, not you, and he's the one who has been supported in the past. Ultimately, the triangle forms because there's a disruption in your relationship with him, and so now you only relate around the authority question, not around the "what hymns do we agree we should sing" question.

Joshua: Yes, I think that's it. As I said, this is a conflict he's had with previous pastors, and I think they each had different reactions. I think Clyde just pointed out he gets to pick the hymns. I hear that didn't go over well. Apparently, the music director became passive-aggressive over that, playing some of the hymns Clyde wanted either too fast or too slow, claiming Clyde could pick the hymns, but he got to pick the tempo.

Graham: Ha, ha, ha! That is so funny!

Joshua: Yeah, as long as it happens to someone else.

Graham: Yes . . . as long as it happens to someone else.

Joshua: With Cindy, I think she just gave him the authority.

Graham: What's your music director's name?

Joshua: You'll love this. It's Isaiah Jeremiah.

Graham: *No!*

Joshua: I kid you not. And I think he sees himself as a prophet.

Graham: Whoa! So, you're contending with a prophet to pick music, and the prophet's used to winning.

Joshua: Uh . . . yup!

Graham: So, the question is how to get out of that triangle.

Joshua: Yeah.

Graham: And your ideas?

Joshua: So far it's been a combination. At certain times I pick the hymns, such as on Sundays that are really important to me, although I can tell he resents it. Other Sundays he picks them if he has a theme going on or if I don't care.

Graham: So, you're slowly going down the Cindy path.

Joshua: Um . . . probably.

Graham: Okay, let's look at alternatives. The issue is how you hold onto your authority without having the prophet feel his is being taken away.

Joshua: That's it.

Graham: I think you have to do a version of what you've been doing with the dysfunctional groups within the church.

Joshua: Like what?

Graham: Well, let me throw out an idea that you don't have to pick up, but it *may* be what I'd do if I were in a similar situation. In fact, it's a variation of what I did with our music director many, many years ago. The key is I wanted to validate his authority while also holding onto mine. With our music director, I created an alliance that allowed us to work together. The idea came from one of my favorite writers on "structural family therapy," Salvador Minuchin. It's a concept he called "marking boundaries."[3] This concept says there's a continuum—a tension—between being enmeshed (where we don't have a self-identity or self-initiative) and disengaged (where we don't have a group identity or work well with others). In some ways, your predecessors were the perfect example of this. Clyde was disengaged, and he set very rigid boundaries. Cindy was enmeshed, and she wanted to bond with everyone emotionally. There's a healthy range in the middle of this continuum we need to strive for, although getting people there can be difficult.

Basically, what he says is if you have a family (or in your case, church) system that is too enmeshed—where people's identities are too engaged with each other—you need to work toward differentiation, helping them develop a self-identity and initiative. As you know, this means you have to help people develop a sense of autonomy that allows them to gain confidence in their abilities away from the group.

So, for instance, if you have an administrative secretary who won't take initiative, you have to push this person to become responsible for work that's independent of you. And you have to praise this person for that work, thus building more confidence.

Meanwhile, if you have someone who's disengaged and too independent, you have to create a sense of collaboration that develops mutuality and integration. Your music director has become too independent from you and everyone else in leadership, but you can't get him to collaborate by taking the authority away from him. You have to find a way to share that authority—to become *interdependent*. You have to push him toward the healthy range.

Joshua: And you have ideas for that?

Graham: Getting there. When I started at my church, I constantly worked with our music director to create a shared, mutual philosophy of our music program. He was a jazz musician who could do classical and contemporary. We spent much time together theorizing on what we needed to do to create a worship service—not a music program but a worship service—that would inspire people.

We spent much time talking about the challenges of reaching a much more diverse musical population. He shared his ideas, I shared mine, and we shared our personal pet peeves about worship, including music. Basically, we forged a worship alliance by creating a mutual, collaborative worship theology and spirituality. We developed a framework that allowed us to work together while also maintaining our authority.

Joshua: How did you end up dealing with hymns?

Graham: We spent a lot of time talking about how to choose hymns. This evolved over the years; but at first, it meant we went over each service by phone to choose what would be the best hymns.

I would share my ideas about the scripture, asking for his help to figure out the best hymns. After a year or so of this, we sat down and actually worked on developing a formula for our three hymns in the service. We agreed the first hymn would always be a more rousing praise hymn. The middle hymn would fit the sermon. The last hymn would be one that felt like a "goodbye" hymn, whatever that means.

Over the years, we shifted our formula as we integrated contemporary music into our service and changed the structure of our worship. We created a new formula. The first hymn would always be contemporary and projected on a screen. The second would always be traditional and out of the hymnal. We called the third hymn the "world" hymn because it's where we might sing gospel, African, folk, or other kinds of hymns that reflect a broader musical scope, one that's more ethnically diverse. We became pretty consistent and developed a high level of trust because we were on the same page spiritually and theologically.

Joshua: Then who chose the hymns?

Graham: Right, sorry. At first we both did. We just scheduled time to talk over the phone. More and more I was coming to him with hymns I thought would work with our formula, but I would always ask if he thought they worked too. Eventually, he didn't mind me making the decision. By the end it was mostly me, but I also felt more comfortable expressing my uncertainty about certain hymns and seeking his guidance. So, if I had an idea for what I wanted, I might pick a hymn, but then call him up and say, "Will this work with what I'm trying to do?" Two times out of three he would say yes, but periodically he'd say, "We just did that a month ago," or "I think this other hymn may work better," or "I hate that hymn!" The point is we created a theology and a system that pushed us to collaborate.

We also got to know each other's likes and dislikes. For example, I would never pick "Shine, Jesus, Shine" unless he was away. Periodically, I'd call him up and say I was thinking of playing song #121 in our songbook. He'd look it up and see "Shine, Jesus, Shine!" and say to me, "You know how I feel about that song." I'd then say, "Yeah, but I was bored and just wanted to hear you get worked up." By then, we had formed a strong relationship, what family therapists call an "alliance." We were working together.

Joshua: Okay, I see what you're saying. If I get into a power struggle for authority with Isaiah, I'll probably end up like Clyde or Cindy. But if I'm willing to work with him so we are sharing authority based on a mutually agreed-upon philosophy, then we break the authority triangle.

Graham: Bingo!

Joshua: What if he won't work with me to create a mutual framework?

Graham: You tell him that for the two of you to do what's best in leading the congregation in worship, you both *have* to be on the same page. Don't threaten his job or anything. Just use your authority as head-of-staff to let him know this is what's expected of a professional church leader. In other words, use your pastoral authority to push him out of the music authority triangle.

Joshua: Let me give you another example. We have a triangle between our trustees and board. The trustees control the money. The board is the elder leaders. There are times when the board will want to develop a particular ministry or mission and the trustees shut it down simply by saying there's not enough money. So, they basically undermine the board's authority.

Graham: I think the same principle applies, but now there are three authorities—the board, the trustees, and you. Perhaps the way through this is to have a retreat for both boards to create a philosophy of budgeting. I didn't have to do this at my church because, thankfully, members of our board were also the trustees. Still, at this retreat, you might teach and do exercises teaching how our God is God, not budgets and affordability. Have them create a philosophy or theology of how to decide what to do. The key is creating a guiding theology the trustees buy into that can guide them.

For instance, you might have them discuss and create a vision for how to balance stretching the church's ministry and mission with the practicalities of what is financially responsible. The key thing I've noticed is often financially responsible people don't want to take risks, and growth in anything requires risk. You may fail. You may lose money. But you may also succeed and find this leads to growth, which leads to more congregational energy, which leads to increased giving. The key is getting them to talk and come to a common understanding.

Detangling the triangle means getting the boards talking to each other and reaching a consensus, rather than having them put you in the middle like a father being asked to pick a favorite child. The elders need to stretch the church. The trustees need to keep the church financially sound. They need to talk with each other about this with your input rather than having you be the go-between.

The retreat idea is one option. It doesn't have to be that elaborate, but it does need to be something that allows them to get on the same page in the decision-making process and gets you out of the middle.

Joshua: Okay, I'm hearing you. What you're saying is that I should create direct talk.

Graham: Yes. That's the basis of systems theory—that direct, healthy, goal-oriented talk leads to healthier relationships and operations.

Joshua: So, how does this relate to another problem, which is the elders *saying* they want to do more mission and ministry but not really wanting to jump on board? They use the trustees' reluctance as an excuse to hold back.

Graham: In other words, they're *ambivalent*. They want to invest more energy without investing more energy. They want more ministry and mission but don't necessarily want to be the drivers of more ministry and mission. You've got an extra dynamic in these triangles where there's a triangle involving the two boards and you, but there's also an *ambivalence triangle* between you and the elders where they use the trustees' reluctance to justify holding back in trying to grow.

Joshua: That's it!

Graham: So how are you trying to motivate them?

Joshua: Oh man! What haven't I tried? I preach about mission a lot, about the need to reach out. I write about it in our monthly newsletters. Even more, I give them all sorts of ideas about mission. I do my research for what we could do both in the community and everywhere else. I've been making it easy for them, and they don't do anything, even though they're constantly telling me how inspiring my passion for mission is.

Graham: And it's amazingly frustrating to have all this passion and all these ideas but get such limited response.

Joshua: Yes, it is.

Graham: Let's move away from triangles for a bit and talk about how you and they function, although it will still be about the triangles. Why are they ambivalent? They're ambivalent because you're over-functioning, and your over-functioning leads both them and you to become burned out. They get burned out because they can't keep up with your passion, and they feel you're just adding more to their already over-functioning lives. They feel guilty for not doing more, but they don't have *your* passion for all *your* ideas. Then *you* get burned out because *you're* over-functioning and *you're* not getting traction. You don't get to do as much of the activities that create meaning and purpose for *you*.

Joshua: Okay, but shouldn't they have more passion?

Graham: Why, because you have it?

Joshua: No, because this is how they serve God. They should have a passion for that. They hired me to stoke the embers of that passion.

Graham: Yeah, I see your point. Let me share what I'm hearing: *They* should have more passion for *your* passion because *your* passion is what God wants *them* to do.

Joshua: No, I just want them to do what God is calling them to do.

Graham: Right, but what I'm hearing is God wants them to do what *you* want them to do.

Joshua: That's not what I mean.

Graham: But it is what you're saying.

Joshua: (crosses arms) I don't mean it that way.

Graham: I know that. In fact, I can see how much you *truly* want them to share your passion.

Joshua: Yes! Is that wrong?

Graham: No, but indulge me for a moment while I tell you the story of Graham, the passionate therapist. Back in the early 1980s, I was working as a therapist with teens in a psychiatric hospital in Virginia. I had a thirteen-year-old patient whose older sister had died of a drug overdose. She had told him at some point before she died that if he didn't let her die in his heart, she'd never really die. I think he took that literally, so he was in a weird denial about her death, thinking his refusal to accept it could lead to her coming back to life.

I didn't know how to deal with all this because I wasn't trained to deal with spiritual issues. In fact, this experience was influential in leading me to go to seminary a few years later while also working on my Master of Social Work. I worked overtime to help this kid. I worked very, very hard, but he wasn't getting much better. I eventually took the case to my supervisor, a PhD clinical psychologist, and we agreed to tape one of my sessions.

After watching twenty minutes, the psychologist clicked off the VHS machine—

Joshua: I've heard about VHS. Didn't they use them back in Jesus's day?

Graham: Very funny. I'd hit you with my old man's cane if I could reach it. Anyway, he said to me, "Graham, you're really working hard. I can tell how much you care." Pridefully I thought to myself, "See, I *am* a good therapist. Maybe one of the best!" I replied, "Yeah, I do work hard with him." He said to me, "That's why he's not getting better. You're doing all the work. Why should he work on his problems when you're so good at working on his problems for him?"

I was stunned. I was no longer the greatest therapist in the world. I. Was. The. Worst! I asked him what I should do. He said, "Just get him thinking about this stuff, and when he's silent for long periods of time, be silent too. He'll eventually talk. And if he doesn't, ask the same question or make the same comment again and let him respond. If he doesn't, then you need to let him be responsible for not working with you."

Joshua: So you're saying . . . ?

Graham: Maybe you're working too hard by giving your church all the ideas for ministry and mission. Maybe you're working so hard you don't leave room for them to be creatively involved in the ministry and mission of the church. Maybe you're not letting them develop their own passions.

117

Joshua: Oh my! Maybe I *am* working too hard. But what about them?

Graham: You asked a question a few minutes ago: "But shouldn't they have the passion?" I think the word "should" can be destructive because it's almost always a judgment on others. How often do we hear "should" in a sentence when it doesn't feel like a judgment? Instead of saying what they should do, ask how can they develop the passion you have if you don't let them develop that passion. How can they do the work of being creative if you are creative for them? Who forced you to be so passionate? Was it someone criticizing you, or did your passions develop over time?

Joshua: (big sigh) I *am* doing all the work for them. I never thought about it that way. And I'm not letting them develop passions. I don't even know what their passions are.

Graham: You do, but you haven't necessarily embraced them. What we've been talking about goes to a principle I've developed in my leadership: *Never work harder than your church.* This goes back to the triangles. When you work harder than them, you break your ministry alliance with them and create a *commitment triangle* around ministry and mission. They're no longer working directly with you because they're busy fighting you in a triangle over ministry and mission. The triangle is you, the congregation, and their willingness or unwillingness to engage in your passions. They have ambivalence about you, and they know they can demonstrate their feelings about you based on whether they engage in the ministries and missions you love.

Frankly, trying not to work so hard with my church is how I started writing books and articles. I had so many ideas early on, but I didn't want to afflict them with all of them. I even kiddingly said to some members, "You don't want me to inflict my full self on you. You won't have the energy to keep up." So, I started writing. Other pastors I know develop hobbies or other interests.

One pastor, who I deeply respect, responded to the same lack of church passion by engaging in personal mission trips to Ghana, regardless of whether the rest of the church followed. He developed a whole personal ministry there that included teaching in a Ghanaian seminary. After years of doing that each year, members of his church and other Presbyterian churches (including ours) started joining him on mission trips to Ghana.

Another pastoral couple I know, who I also deeply respect, sensed a call to lead people on a trip to Israel every year. It didn't matter if those on the trip came from their churches or not. They just felt it was their personal calling. I went on one of their trips two years ago, and it was the most amazing trip I've ever taken.

Joshua: Okay, I'm getting this. I'm creating power-struggle triangles around my passions rather than letting congregants develop their own passions. I need to tone down my interests so they can creatively develop theirs.

Graham: Sort of, but not to that extreme. You need to temper your passions so the church can become more passionate, which hopefully will allow them to begin embracing your passions. Here's the rub: what if they develop passions for things you don't care as much about? Are you willing to help them discern and listen for God's call in their lives rather than what *you believe* is God's call in their lives? Are you willing to help them develop passions you're not passionate about? In the meantime, if you can't completely fulfill your passion in your church, can you look for other ways of doing it? That gives you the patience to let them grow.

Joshua: I'm going to have to figure out how to do this. It's not the way I've been doing things.

Graham: I know. Imagine how hard it was for me to not work so hard with my patient. Or all my other patients. Or my church.

Joshua: Any tips on this that you learned?

Graham: You'll figure it out as long as you remember loving them means helping them grow at their pace for their own callings.

Joshua: Can you give me a couple more "for instances" of what you mean?

Graham: Yeah. We had a huge drama mission at our church. I didn't share their passion for drama, but I did everything I could to help them with their passions. While I was there, our drama ministry went from offering one adult musical a year to an adult one and a teen one. We upgraded the sound and lighting for them, which also meant upgrading sound and lighting for the sanctuary, since the plays took place in our sanctuary. I did a lot behind the scenes to help that happen, but it was their passion, not mine.

Also, I don't like contemporary Christian worship music, but the church was developing a greater passion for integrating contemporary-style music. So, behind the scenes and in front, I worked on getting us projection systems, creating a process where we could add musicians and the like.

Other areas—at several points we offered divorce ministries or singles ministries in the church because members of our pastoral staff had a passion for that. They offered Friday evening dances and singles' outings. These definitely weren't my passion, but I worked to help them. I supported their work.

If it's okay, I'll let those examples settle in. We don't have much time and I want to circle back to talking about systems theory.

Joshua: Sure.

Graham: Here's the key thing I learned from my studies in family systems, especially in working with couples and families and trying hard to *not* work harder than them. Ultimately, we can fill our heads with thoughts of triangles, coalitions, alliances, dysfunction, homeostasis, and the rest. In the end, though, you have to break it all down into the one primary thing all systems theory is about: *relationships*.

Systems theory is not about doing this thing over here to get people to that thing over there. It's not a theory meant to help you manipulate things to achieve your ambitions. Systems theory is *always* about nurturing healthier, more direct, collaborative relationships. It's about helping people form relationships based on mutuality, respect, cooperation, collaboration, and compassion. The more that's the focus, the more intuitive systems theory becomes. You can't get there by criticizing, coercing, manipulating, or conspiring.

When it comes to the church, the focus is on how you, as their pastor and leader, can help them become healthier in their relationships with each other. Don't become so obsessed with triangles, and with trying to snoop them out, that you forget the relationships.

Joshua: That's very helpful. I think I forget the relationships a lot.

I think I focus so much on getting them to do things, I forget to care about them. All I can think of is how they're not helping *me* do the ministry and mission I want.

Graham: So, what do you do now?

Joshua: I'm not quite sure yet. I think you're right, but I still feel we need to change the system.

Graham: You do, but it has to be grounded in forming healthier relationships everywhere—with each other, with you, with God, with the community. If your focus is on *fixing* the system, then it won't work in the end. I already said this, but if you forget the relationships in the midst of trying to change them, you'll lose the whole purpose of church, which is nurturing loving relationships with God, each other, and themselves. It's the Great Command: "You shall love the Lord your God with all your heart, and with all your soul, and with all your strength, and with all your mind; and your neighbor as yourself."[4]

Joshua: I'm hearing that pretty clearly.

Graham: And you're getting tired.

Joshua: Yes, and my head's spinning a bit.

Graham: You did good work today—more work than I did because you're going home with it. (laughs)

Joshua: Yep, and I promise to work harder than you on this.

Graham: Good. Then I'll give you homework to do.

Joshua: Okay.

Graham: I want you to take some paper and look at all the areas you may be over-functioning. List them. And then reflect on them and write out how you can step back to *healthy* functioning. Don't go to under-functioning, but explore *healthy* functioning.

Joshua: Can we go over this next time?

Graham: Absolutely.

FURTHER THOUGHTS

Having been trained as a marital and family therapist causes me to look at systems theory in a different light from those like Edwin Friedman who have adapted it to organizational theory. They tend to focus on how to help organizations become more cohesive and effective, whereas therapy is always focused on forging healthier relationships. Now "healthy" may not mean staying married. It may focus on how to forge a healthy separation to test the waters. For example, the focus may be on how to engage in a healthy divorce that creates the healthiest context for the children, rather than creating conflict triangles where the children become chess pieces in a game of "defeat the spouse." Likewise, it can mean how to forge a healthier marriage that will endure many years ahead. The key is cultivating a relationship that reflects a level of mutuality, respect, and collaboration. Systems thinking offers an amazing perspective on organizational and congregational life, but it is at its strongest when the focus is on nurturing healthy relationships and not just nurturing good decision-making.

I've noticed two significant leadership obstacles arising from the ways pastors and congregational leaders typically perceive their churches. These obstacles arise because pastors adopt a perspective that interferes with their ability to recognize the systemic processes going on in their churches. The first problematic perception is some pastors see church as *a collection of individuals who are always vying for influence and control.* Pastors and leaders who operate from this perspective, even if only slightly, tend to lead anxiously because they fear someone with power or influence will sabotage or undermine their leadership. It's an exhausting perspective rooted in self-protection.

Over the years, I've gotten to know many pastors who anxiously lead a collection of individuals. They often create conflict precisely because their fear of conflict nurtures conflict. They often hold a hierarchical view of church members, fearing those perceived to have power and treating them with deference and respect, and they disregard those perceived to have little power. In their minds, they put individuals on a ladder of power and influence and then treat them accordingly. Conflict arises as these pastors act self-protectively against perceived threats. Even more, conflict arises because they fear relationships.

For example, an interim pastor I know who has a history of conflict met with the program and support staff soon after coming to the church. The interim saw the previous pastor as a threat, so he called a meeting where he said, "You will have no contact with the previous pastor whatsoever." It was his way of getting the staff on his side, as if there were sides to choose. Of course, within hours the staff were calling the previous pastor about this. The interim feared the influence of the previous pastor and reacted self-protectively in a way that created conflict. He established a triangle where the staff had to choose whom they would support: the pastor who was involved in hiring them, with whom they had forged years of relationships; or the one they had just met who was only going to be temporary. This conflict led the staff to dislike him from the start.

Pastors who see the church as a collection of individuals have a hard time with systems thinking because it requires stepping out of our personal perspective to move to a different metalevel and see a greater context—an organizational and even organic system in which everyone plays a significant role, no matter how insignificant they may seem. Something family systems theory developer Salvador Minuchin said about family systems can easily be applied to congregational systems (with apologies for its overly masculine language):

> The theory of family therapy is predicated on the fact that man is not an isolate. He is an acting and reacting member of social groups. What he experiences as real depends on both internal and external components . . . Man's experience is determined by his interaction with his environment.[5]

I have no proof of this, but I suspect pastors who see churches as collections of individuals are most likely to be pushed out of the church as more and more people without power complain and gain the power of influence to make that happen. These pastors have forgotten churches are communities of relationships, and the healthier the relationships, the healthier the communities. Seeing churches as a collection of individuals degrades the ability to create relationships.

Churches aren't just a collection of individuals within a congregation. They are simultaneously *both* individuals and parts of larger communities. To create healthier systems, the focus has to be on nurturing healthy relationships. When we use systems theory to manipulate and get what we want, we break down relationships. To build healthy congregational systems, we have to create healthy structures. We need to structure boards, committees, worship, events, groups, and everything else with a mind toward developing healthy relationships *with each other*. The more we're able to create healthy interactions at all levels, the healthier the congregations will be.

Thus, boards, committees, task forces, teams, etc. need to be seen primarily as relational groups, not production groups. Committees, boards, teams, and task forces are significant avenues through which church members build relationships with each other. What they accomplish is actually secondary in healthy churches. So, the board leader who demands efficiency and adheres to a strict polity and reliance on rules of order inhibits relationships. Things may get done, but relationships break down over time. Power struggles ensue. Reaching consensus becomes not only difficult, but also irrelevant. All that matters is achieving a 51 percent vote that moves motions forward.

In healthy churches, the "how" is more important than the "what." Years ago, we had a situation where a task force of two members was created to investigate ways to repair the front steps and porch of the church. Each was committed to different proposals and wanted the board to choose between them. I sat down with the two and said I wouldn't let either proposal go to the board because I cared much more about *how* they decided what to do than about *what* they decided. I also said I cared much more about their relationships, and the church's relationships, than about the front steps. My instructions were for them to find a way to create one proposal, to work together. Within a week, they did this by merging their two proposals. In so doing, they also created bonds that allowed the board to go forward as one body in sync with each other. They didn't become best friends, but they became more connected with each other in a way that allowed the church board to act in a relationally healthy way.

A second obstacle arising out of how pastors perceive their church is *viewing it as a single organism*. This is the opposite of the first. They lose the individuals as they continually refer to "the church," as in "the church said they don't want to engage in this kind of mission," or "the church said it only wants traditional hymns." In actuality, they don't see the church as a single organism. They see those resisting their leadership as speaking for "the church," and so their leadership becomes timid and overly deferential. It lacks courage and conviction. These pastors will push a church forward as long as there's not too much resistance rather than working to overcome the resistance to move them forward.

The *systems* mistake pastors make from this perspective is they give too much power to those creating the most noise—the group that pushes back the hardest. They see their leadership as "me," the pastor versus "the church," with "me" often losing. They want to lead the church forward, but their anxieties continually cause them to look for how the church is subverting their authority.

Again, no proof of this, but my experience says these are the kinds of pastors who are most likely to leave churches after a relatively short stay of three to four years in their ongoing search for "the church" that will accept their leadership and go along with their ideas. They aren't pushed out, but they do opt out.

Healthy leadership entails the ability to see a church as both a collection of atoms and a galaxy at the same time. As Peter Steinke says:

> A system is a collection of parts that connect and interact. Systems range from the cellular to the solar, from an auto's cooling system to the city's transit system, from genes to groups. The bits and pieces by themselves tell us little about a system's functioning. We need to see how the bits and pieces act on one another.[6]

To regard any part of the church as "the church" is a significant problem for leaders because it cedes the authority of leadership to those who resist growth, risk, and transformation the most. Sometimes, leading is a matter of moving forward regardless of the complaints.

We can change the system and the church, but only if the purpose is to create a church of healthy relationships—with God, others, and self—that lead to ministry and mission. Again, the secret sauce for leading forward despite "the church's" complaining lies in nurturing healthier relationships. For instance, a *resistance triangle* can arise where pastors become obsessed with the church's "resisting" their ideas while the church becomes obsessed with the best ways to resist their ideas. As long as resistance becomes the wedge between a pastor and the resisting part of the congregation, it never resolves itself. It only resolves itself as the pastor remains in healthy relationship with the resisters despite their disagreement, since the pastor refuses to let the resistance cause them to avoid, and even become defensive around, the resisters.

For instance, early in my ministry at Calvin Presbyterian Church, we had an elder who didn't like many of my ideas. He was also the chair of our Building and Property Committee. So, any of my ideas that involved the building or the property had to go through his committee. I had minor tussles with him over how to move forward. He severely resisted adding internet to the church, opposed spending more money to hire a separate custodian when our previous secretary/treasurer/custodian moved away (yes, one person did all three jobs), and always wanted to accept the cheapest solution even if, in the long run, it led to constant, ongoing repairs that cost more money than a first, more expensive repair would have. He looked at me as a soft-handed, lofty-minded guy who didn't understand practical things.

I knew he didn't think much about me when it came to building and property matters, despite the fact I actually did have a good understanding of things. It was a power struggle in the making. But I never let it be. I realized he didn't speak for the church, but that he represented a minority of older people like him who struggled to adapt to a changing church culture. I saw him neither as a saboteur nor as "the church." I simply saw him as a person whose trust

I needed to gain. So instead of treating him as a threat, I constantly met with him to talk over minor property matters, even if I could have taken care of them myself. If there was a repair he was making, I would be with him and have him show me what he was doing. I would seek him out especially when I knew he disagreed with me. I would validate his views, even if I disagreed.

On the issue of the internet, I had him meet me in my office and I showed him how it could work. I didn't win him over. His response to the newfangled possibility of emailing bulletin stuff to the secretary was, "Why don't you just walk over to her office and give her the stuff?" I said, "Because in five years, everyone's going to have internet, and people will work more from home. This is how we'll communicate. Vic, I respect how you can fix anything and how you're teaching me how to take care of the building. Please respect that this is an area I understand." It's hard now to believe his resistance in an age where all business seems to be done through email and instant messaging. Anyway, he eventually—crankily—came on board because of our wary, yet relatively solid relationship.

Ultimately, my point throughout this whole chapter is church systems can be changed, but only if we recognize that these systems are built on relationships. Whatever the organizational, systemic perspective we adhere to in church leadership, we have to remember it's all built on healthy relationships. If our goal isn't relational and mainly to achieve our pastoral ambitions, then we'll find that no level of systemic understanding will lead to real systemic change that lasts.

The following exercise may help you to identify the areas where you may unwittingly become trapped by triangles, and to explore how to create better relationships by changing the systems.

RELATIONAL TRIANGLES REFLECTION

All of us live in communities of interlocking triangles. We can't escape them. They're everywhere. They exist in marital arguments over who should take out the trash; friendship confusions over whether to split the dinner check; work discussions on who should make a presentation; and boozy arguments over politics. The key isn't avoiding triangles. It is in recognizing when the triangles have become dysfunctional, disrupting relationships, and then figuring out what to do about them.

The previous section described two perspectives pastors can hold that unwittingly create or exacerbate dysfunctional triangles. In the following, reflect on how you may tend toward a particular perspective, how this perspective can contribute to forming dysfunctional triangles in your congregation, and what you can do to develop healthier relationships leading to healthier communities.

Church as a Collection of Individuals Always Vying for Influence and Control

- In what ways have you regarded your congregation as a collection of individuals, and how has that impacted your leadership? Describe a concrete example.
- How has regarding your congregation in this way contributed to dysfunctional triangles? Use the concrete example above as a way of exploring this. Draw a triangle with you; the person or group you feel you've been vying with; and the issue, event, or idea you may be triangulating.
- How can you respond differently in ways that dismantle the dysfunctional triangles and create healthier relationships throughout the system? Again, use the concrete example to describe how you might respond differently.

Church as a Single Organism

- In what ways have you regarded your congregation as a single organism, and how has that impacted your leadership? Write down a concrete example of this.
- How has regarding your congregation in this way contributed to dysfunctional triangles? Use the concrete example above as a way of exploring this. Draw a triangle with you; the person or group you feel you've been vying with; and the issue, event, or

idea you may be triangulating.

- How can you respond differently in ways that dismantle the dysfunctional triangles and create healthier relationships throughout the system? Again, use the concrete example as a strategy for responding differently.

NOTES

1. Edwin H. Friedman, *Generation to Generation: Family Process in Church and Synagogue* (New York: The Guilford Press, 1985).

2. Actual quote: "If a leader will take primary responsibility for his or her own position as 'head' and work to define his or her own goals and self, while *staying in touch* with the rest of the organism, there is a more than reasonable chance that the body will follow. There may be initial resistance but, if the leader can stay in touch with the resisters, the body will usually go along." Friedman, *Generation to Generation*, 229.

3. Salvador Minuchin, *Families and Family Therapy* (Cambridge, MA: Harvard University Press, 1974), 143–47.

4. Luke 10:27.

5. Minuchin, *Families and Family Therapy*, 2.

6. Peter L. Steinke, *Healthy Congregations: A Systems Approach* (Lanham, MD: Rowman & Littlefield, 2006), 6.

6

GOD ACTUALLY *IS* WITH YOU!

Dawn is a Presbyterian pastor in her fourth year at a mostly suburban church outside of Pittsburgh, Pennsylvania. Prior to her leadership, the church had experienced a twenty-year decline. Despite the decline, Dawn came to the church because she felt it had a great spirit and the members seemed to be very loving toward others—both within and outside of the church. The church listed spiritual growth as one of its primary interests when seeking a new pastor, and this quality fit with what Dawn was seeking in a church.

In her four years at the church, she has focused on teaching different spiritual practices, such as contemplative prayer, journaling, sabbath-keeping, tithing, and others. Also, she has developed many special weekday worship services throughout the year that are rooted in Taizé chanting, walking a labyrinth, and Lectio Divina, as well as offering yearly spiritual retreats and periodic classes focused on spiritual practices.

She is frustrated because she thought an emphasis on these practices would yield more growth and stoke the church's passion for outreach to those who've walked away from the church—especially those who call themselves "spiritual but not religious." The growth has been marginal. While the church is more active and has grown slightly during her four years, it's not what she anticipated. Also, she's frustrated because only a relatively small percentage of the church has been involved in some or all of these practices.

She got in touch with me because she had read my book Becoming a

Blessed Church and thought I might be able to help her figure out what she's missing in her ministry. Specifically, she feels the growth has been a slog and is wondering what she can do to make God more present for people.

This is our sixth meeting together. Previous meetings focused on her concerns about things that aren't working as well as she had hoped, and on exploring different avenues that might create the vibrancy she's sought.

****

Dawn: I came close to not coming today. I've been thinking over what we've talked about, and I'm worried we keep moving around in circles, that I'm wasting your time talking about frustrations repeatedly.

Graham: I'm glad you came anyway. I enjoy our conversations because they're very close to so much of what I've had to work through in my own ministry to figure out how to create a more spiritually vibrant church.

Dawn: Good, because I've been struggling with something you said last time. It's been bothering me. You said something like, "Churches don't grow because of practices. They grow because of their connection with God." I think I was irritated by that because, as you know, I've been working pretty hard at creating a church that integrates spiritual practices into its ministry so we can connect with God. I sort of felt like you were saying everything I was doing was wrong.

Graham: Oh my gosh. I'm so sorry about that. I don't think you heard it the way I meant it, but I'm glad you came back. What I said wasn't meant as a criticism. I was sharing what I had experienced in my ministry, both before and after I went to Calvin Presbyterian Church.

Dawn: What do you mean "before"? Did you do spiritual ministry in a church before then? I thought you didn't do that until after you got your PhD.

Graham: Much of what I did at Calvin Church was based on experiences I had before coming there. I don't mean my studies. I mean my experiences.

Dawn: Which were . . . ?

Graham: I started doing spiritual small groups and classes while I was an associate pastor in another church, which went well. I also gained more experiences while working full-time on my PhD through the retreats and classes I led on prayer and spirituality in many churches. Like you, much of what I taught was basic Christian spiritual practices.

What impacted my thinking, and eventually my approach at Calvin Church, was the feedback I got from pastors after my retreats and classes. They always said the members loved the classes and retreats, but they had hoped the lessons taught in there would spread more into the rest of the church. When I asked the reason why they thought the spiritual teachings didn't spread more, they said it was because too many felt the spiritual practices I taught weren't practical enough or were too hard to engage in regularly. That got me thinking more deeply about whether teaching individual members prayer practices, Lectio Divina, contemplation, and other spiritual practices was enough to help the whole church become deeper spiritually.

Dawn: I think I'm experiencing a bit of that too. I had hoped doing all these practices would spread.

Graham: And they haven't.

Dawn: And they haven't.

Graham: And that's been your primary frustration?

Dawn: I think so. I think I thought opening them up spiritually would make things easier and would lead to more growth.

Graham: What I've learned is it doesn't necessarily make things easier. In fact, nurturing spirituality in a church often makes things harder.

Dawn: Why?

Graham: Because being more spiritually aware and alive is very difficult for people who've been spiritually unaware and asleep.

Dawn: But shouldn't engaging them in spiritual practices make them more aware and awake?

Graham: It depends. Members of most modern churches haven't been steeped in the spiritual—whether it's spiritual practices or thinking. They've been steeped in religious rituals and events. They've been steeped in theological thinking and beliefs. But they haven't necessarily been steeped in a spiritual awareness of God's presence. They'll talk about God's presence from an intellectual standpoint, but few have truly and deeply experienced God's presence regularly. In fact, I think much of our theological and religious talk about God's presence serves as an arm's-length substitute for the intimate experience of God's presence.

Dawn: I get that. I think that's why I wanted to develop all these practices. I wanted people to experience God through the practices, just as I experienced God through them.

Graham: Yeah, but see, this is where I'm wondering if that's the case.

Dawn: That I've experienced God through practices?

Graham: No, that your primary experiences of God have come through the practices. I think your secondary experiences of God have come through practices. I think your primary experiences have come through other experiences that then led you to want more, which then led you to become interested in practices.

Dawn: Ummm . . . my experiences led me to become interested in practices. Actually, a practice *did* lead me to experience God and go to seminary.

Graham: Really? I may challenge that, but tell me what you mean.

Dawn: Well, I was struggling with whether I should become a pastor ten years ago. I was working in a laboratory doing testing and was wondering if I should be doing something more meaningful. I was *really* struggling with it. I felt much more meaning in the volunteering I did at the church. They had a spiritual retreat led by a professor from the local seminary. It was during a prayer walk she had us do that I had a deep experience of God saying, "Be like her."

Graham: So, you felt God saying to be a professor?

Dawn: No, she was a pastor first. I heard God saying to be like her as a pastor. Those are the kinds of experiences I want other people to have.

Graham: Right, but that experience was secondary.

Dawn: No, it was my primary experience.

Graham: No, your primary experience was your dissatisfaction with your work, your passion for volunteering at your church, your wondering if there was something more, and your sense you should be part of that retreat. In essence, God was already whispering to you. You were already experiencing God's presence and sensing God's guidance through your volunteering, praying, study, and church involvement before the retreat. You just noticed the secondary experience more. You were already becoming awake and aware. What the prayer walk did was to make you aware you were waking up. The alarm had already rung. You were no longer hitting the snooze button. The prayer walk was simply you getting out of bed.

Dawn: Wow! I hadn't thought of it that way. So, the practices sharpened the experiences I was already having.

Graham: Yes. The prayer walk was an experience, but it built upon the other experiences. This relates to your church struggles. Growing a church based solely on cultivating spiritual practices doesn't necessarily cultivate the underlying experiences the practices nurture. As a result, members don't always feel compelled to do the practices.

The struggle in our churches is our members tend to live functional lives, rather than spiritual lives, six days of the week. Their spiritual connection is mostly nurtured through the church, but they aren't at the church that much. So, they slide back into functionality over the course of the week. As a friend once said to me, "I notice when I get to my office in the morning, I hang up my jacket along with my spirituality. I put both back on at 5:00 p.m. when I leave work." The practices by themselves aren't enough to compel people to nurture a deeper spirituality. That comes through experiences that then motivate them to want to go deeper.

Here's the thing: they won't want to do studies, they won't want to spend time in prayer, they won't want to journal, they won't want to go on retreats or take your classes unless they've already had some level of experience with God that opens them up to wanting more.

Dawn: Well. I'm screwed, then, because I have no idea how to manufacture the experience.

Graham: Ha! Yes, if it were left up to us. But it's not. You don't have to manufacture the experiences. You're only responsible for creating a culture and ethos where experiencing God is not only okay, but also encouraged. When you permit people to recognize and normalize their experiences, they become self-motivated to seek more.

Dawn: And you do that how, if you're not going to do practices?

Graham: I didn't say get rid of the practices. They're an important part of the culture and ethos. What I said is to create a culture and ethos that nurture experience first. The practices are crucial but secondary. Focus primarily on the experiences of God rather than the practices, but still offer the practices as opportunities to deepen these experiences.

Dawn: So, did you have practices at your church?

Graham: Absolutely, but they weren't the focus. This is getting difficult to explain because it's reversed from the way we've all been thinking about spirituality. The Buddhists have a saying: "When pointing at the moon, don't focus on the finger." In other words, the moon is the focus, not the finger. Spiritual intimacy with God and spiritual growth are the focus, not the practices. The experiences are the moon. The practices are the finger.

At our church, we offered many, many practices. We had a permanent labyrinth outside. We had several spiritual small groups for members to read and discuss deep spiritual books—one is still going twenty years later, another eighteen years later. We had a weekly prayer group that prayed for requests, the church, the members, the staff, themselves, and the world. We had monthly prayer vigils for anyone to drop by for prayer. We offered two contemplative prayer groups. We offered several different kinds of Bible studies. We offered holy yoga one morning a week. We offered healing prayer for those in need. Those are the things I remember off the top of my head. The key, though, is none of these practices was the focus. Spiritual growth and connection with God were.

Dawn: Okay. I think I'm grasping this. You're not saying the practices are bad. You're saying the practices have to serve the growth and relationship with Christ, so the practices you offer aren't as important as what they can help us do.

Graham: Yes, which then helps us look at church in multidimensional ways—so everything we do can also be a spiritual practice. Worship becomes a practice, coffee after church becomes a practice, classes become a practice. Everything becomes a practice.

We intentionally offered a whole slew of practices because not everyone's built the same. The person who may resonate with walking the labyrinth may not be able to sit for thirty minutes in contemplative prayer. The person who likes the more evangelical Bible study may not resonate with a group that's reading and reflecting on books by Thomas Merton, Thomas Kelly, Thomas à Kempis, Thomas Keating, or a bunch of other people named Thomas.

Dawn: Wait, you have a group based just on people named Thomas?

Graham: No, that was my bad joke. It's just many spiritual writers have been named Thomas. The groups also read books by Henri Nouwen, Philip Yancey, Richard Foster, Dorotheus of Gaza, Corrie ten Boom, *The Way of a Pilgrim, The Philokalia,* and many others.

Dawn: I know some of them, but not a lot. I get your point, though. It's offering practices and opportunities for the experience that matters.

Graham: Yes. The irony is the Christian church on Pentecost was founded on a dramatic spiritual experience, but the modern church resists spiritual experiences. Can you imagine what people would think if you came into church one day and said, "Guess what? I had the most amazing experience yesterday. I was in a room with several others, praying. Suddenly a wind began to blow, flames appeared over all our heads, and we began speaking in different languages."

Dawn: They'd think we're crazy!

Graham: They would, yet that's our founding church experience. I think in many ways, our mainline Protestant churches have become like secular-religious gatherings where we're a bit scared of actually experiencing God. We'd rather keep God at arm's length. In fact, I think this is a reason Pentecostal and evangelical churches have grown while we've shrunk. Whatever kind of criticism we can lay on them, they've emphasized the experience of God.

Dawn: I think you're hitting what I'm struggling with. I want to help people have an experience of God. Maybe not as passionate as the one from Pentecost, but experiences. My thought has been that having many practices, or figuring out what *one* practice might work best, would lead to experience. What you're saying is the experiences lead us to the practices, which then nurture further experiences. And creating a culture where it's okay to have God-experiences nurtures interest in the practices.

Graham: Yes.

Dawn: So, where does discernment fit into all of this?

Graham: What do you mean?

Dawn: You've written and taught a lot about discernment. If you don't have a practice, how do you get them to discern . . . sorry . . . if the practice of discernment isn't the main thing, how do you get them to discern?

Graham: That's where thinking in 3-D helps.

Dawn: 3-D?

Graham: Three-dimensional discernment. We tend to think one-dimensionally about discernment. We think, "Give me the one practice that will allow me to hear God." So, you'll emphasize the need to sit in silence for five minutes. Or you'll set up a process of alternating reflections and meditations with silence. Or you'll do something you hope will lead to listening to God. That's thinking one-dimensionally—do this to get that. Discerning three-dimensionally means integrating practices like those but doing much more.

For me, it's about everything we do in a church. I'm struck that the Bible never tells you how people heard God, only that they heard God. The Bible doesn't seem interested in instructing us how to hear God. It treats it as though hearing God is the most natural thing in the world. I think it's meant to be. The problem is when we think one-dimensionally, we get trapped into thinking that by engaging in *this* practice, we should be able to hear God in *that* way. And so, we miss how God is speaking to us in other ways.

Dawn: So, how did you get your church to become a discerning church?

Graham: I made it part of everything we did. I once told our associate pastor I must preach on discernment at least ten times a year, but each time I'd do it differently because each time focuses on a different aspect of discernment. I might preach about how to hear God as God speaks through Scripture, others, television shows, podcasts, music, art, poetry, nature, and everything else in life. But I also might preach on how to become humble so we can put aside our egos to hear God, or how to put aside our emotions so we can hear God's deeper guidance. Or how to use silence. Or how to adopt a gratitude practice that develops a sensitivity to God. Or how to be aware of God's presence everywhere.

I also teach classes on different aspects of prayer and discernment at least once every two or three years. But in between, I teach classes on topics that support discernment. I've taught classes on the Enneagram, Myers-Briggs, and understanding ourselves psychologically. I've taught classes on forgiveness, grace, healing, Christian mysticism, how to read the Bible in a more spiritually reflective way, and understanding John's Gospel—which is a deeply spiritual Gospel. I've also taught classes on great spiritual writers, such as Henri Nouwen and Thomas Merton, and their insights.

We've also set up small groups focused on reading spiritual writings that span the ages. I've mentioned this before, but you can find free resources, including bibliographies, for setting these up on my website, ngrahamstandish.org. And we offered yearly spiritual retreats. That gets us to being two-dimensional.

What made us three-dimensional is we set up processes and agendas for our board, committees, and task forces that always included time for studies related to discernment. In fact, you can find a three-year cycle of free, downloadable studies I created for boards and committees on my website. All the quotes in the studies are related to discernment in one way or another. In essence, we made discernment central to the whole church culture. That's what made us three-dimensional. I think you've read about much of that in *Becoming a Blessed Church*.

Dawn: I have, but this makes me understand how comprehensive it is. I keep looking for the one thing I can do to make them more discerning. What you're saying is I have to get them to make listening and following Christ part of the whole culture.

Graham: Yes, but I'll have you take a step back. You first have to make it central to your life too. If you aren't working on making discernment central to your own life, then it won't be part of theirs. You can only lead them to what you've experienced.

Dawn: Okay, I'm seeing that.

Graham: Actually, I have another thought I want to share. Sorry for going on and on; I'm worried I'm not letting you talk much.

Dawn: It's okay. I'm not just here to talk. I'm here to learn, and you've done these things in your ministry.

Graham: So, it's okay if I keep going?

Dawn: Yeah.

Graham: Here's another thought I think is central. We're talking about fundamentally helping a church become deeply awake and aware. This is something the great spiritual writer Anthony de Mello talks a lot about in his book *Awareness*.[1] He says real spirituality is about awareness and awakening to God's presence everywhere. Awareness and awakening start with you. The more consistently you're aware of God, the more alert you'll be to God's presence, and the more you'll be able to wake others.

Dawn: So, discernment's really about awareness of God's presence.

Graham: Yes! That's it! And you're the constant alarm clock waking people up by pointing out that God is there and there, and there, and there, and there. Let me share a quote for you from this book over here. Give me a second. (reaches for a book on a bookshelf) This book is by Thomas Merton. It's small, but it's great. You can see it's called *Thoughts in Solitude*. He talks about being aware. I'll make a copy of this for you, but I'd encourage you to get a copy of this book. Listen to what he says:

> To keep ourselves spiritually alive we must constantly renew our faith. We are like pilots of fog-bound steamers, peering into

the gloom in front of us, listening for the sounds of other ships, and we can only reach our harbor if we keep alert. The spiritual life is, then, first a matter of keeping awake. We must not lose our sensitivity to spiritual inspirations. We must always be able to respond to the slightest warnings that speak, as though by a hidden instinct, in the depth of the soul that is spiritually alive.[2]

What do you hear in all of this?

Dawn: This is a lot. What I'm hearing is I have to be like the pilot of the fog-bound steamer for my congregation. I have to be the one peering into the gloom, listening for God's voice that guides us through the mists. But I also have to train them to listen too. And this is more than just teaching them a discipline or practice of discernment. It's also helping them apply it naturally to all of life.

Graham: Yes.

Dawn: This helps. You wrote about some of this in one of your chapters in the new version of *Becoming a Blessed Church*.[3] What I'm hearing is it's okay to teach practices of discernment, but a church that discerns is one that is increasingly aware of God throughout the life of the congregation. And that starts with me being aware of God.

Graham: Yep, and if I had said it so succinctly earlier, you wouldn't have had to sit and listen to me yap for the past twenty minutes.

Dawn: No, it's good. It's getting me thinking about how I can change my preaching, how to teach this, and how to create groups around this.

Graham: Good. I have one more thing we did to help our congregation. Two, actually. I listened as people shared their experiences of God and often would get permission to use these stories in my sermons, which included identifying them when I told their stories. I wanted congregants to know that people in the pews with them were having these experiences. I wanted to normalize the experiences. Over years of listening, I also asked people to write down their experiences. Twice we collected and edited what they wrote and turned their accounts into Lenten resources we called "Calvin

Stories." We shared them with the congregation. We couldn't print enough. When we put out "Calvin Stories 2" in 2011, we made about 500 copies, and everyone grabbed them up as quickly as we put them out. People shared them with family and friends. Our membership was only about 400-something at the time. We couldn't print them fast enough.

Dawn: That's such a cool idea. Did anyone object to having you tell these stories in your sermons?

Graham: Nope. Actually, many said it was very helpful because then they could talk to these folks about their experiences.

Dawn: I have to think about all that. I have another burning, bummer question. What if it feels like God isn't listening or responding? What if you get a congregation listening, but they don't hear anything?

Graham: Scrooge! Just kidding. That's a *very* good question. It goes into part of the Christian spiritual tradition that too few Christians know. I may be about to go on for another yapping session, so I'll apologize ahead of time. I don't know how to talk about it without talking about it in its fullness.

There's a strain of Christian spirituality that's not only built on the awareness that de Mello talked about, but is also about more than this awareness. It's about what Jesus taught when he talked about the vine and the branches. He said, "I am the vine, you are the branches. Those who abide in me and I in them bear much fruit, because apart from me you can do nothing."[4]

I don't like the translation of "abide." I think a better word would be to say "live," as in, "those who live in me and I in them bear much fruit." What do you hear in this passage?

Dawn: That we're connected to Christ.

Graham: There's more. What must the branch do to bear fruit?

Dawn: Ummm . . . I guess blossom.

Graham: But the blossoming occurs naturally. What does it actually have to *do* to let that blossoming naturally occur?

Dawn: Stay connected to the vine?

Graham: Bingo! And that's what allows the sap, or God's grace, to naturally flow through us and allow us to bear fruit. This particular understanding of how God works is fundamental to this strain of Christian spirituality I'm sharing.

Dawn: Staying connected to the vine.

Graham: Yeah. When we ask, "What if God doesn't respond?" we're disconnecting from the vine. What happens is all of our anxieties and doubts make us try to gain control over everything instead of trusting God with the results. It's something a great Quaker spiritual writer, Hannah Whitall Smith, talks about in her book *The Christian's Secret to a Happy Life*. (reaches for the book) I have it right here on my desk. In 1875, she wrote about how to connect with God and let go of anxieties. I'll make a copy of this quote for you. She says:

> To sum it all up, then, what is needed for happy and effectual service is simply to put your work into the Lord's hands, and leave it there. Do not take it to Him in prayer, saying, "Lord, guide me; Lord, give me wisdom; Lord, arrange it for me," and then rise from your knees, and take the burden all back and try to guide and arrange for yourself. *Leave* it with the Lord; and remember that what you trust to Him you must not worry over nor feel anxious about. Trust and worry cannot go together. If your work is a burden it is because you are not trusting it to Him. But if you do trust it to Him you will surely find that the yoke He puts on you is easy, and the burden He gives you to carry is light: and even in the midst of a life of ceaseless activity you shall "find rest to your soul."[5]

Dawn: I need to take that quote with me and think about it. I hear what she's saying, though, which is when we get nervous about God not being there, we disconnect.

Graham: Yes. Smith is part of a Christian spiritual tradition that's fully based on abandonment to God and allowing God's grace to flow through everything we do. It's a tradition of divine providence you find peeking out here and there throughout Christian history, and the dominant Christian tradition never knows what to do with it—in the same way they don't know what to do with Pentecost or the miracles of the Bible.

These are Christian writers, such as the fourteenth-century German mystic Meister Eckhart; the Quaker writer Thomas Kelly; the evangelical writer Frank Laubach; the seventeenth-century monk Brother Lawrence; the Presbyterian writer Catherine Marshall; the twentieth-century Anglican writer Evelyn Underhill; the nineteenth-century evangelical preacher George Müller and his twenty-first-century counterpart Henry Blackaby; the Episcopal writer on healing, Agnes Sanford; the Dutch Christian Holocaust survivor Corrie ten Boom; and so many more.

They all talk about this spiritual relationship between us and God that allows coincidences, providences, and God-incidences to happen all the time. One of my favorite quotes on this, which I try to keep at the forefront of my awareness, came from the early twentieth-century Archbishop of Canterbury, William Temple. This is from memory, but he said something like, "I notice that when I pray, coincidences happen. When I stop praying, coincidences stop happening."[6]

Ultimately, what they're saying is God is actually with you.

Dawn: And you've experienced this?

Graham: All throughout my ministry. So many coincidences have happened in my life that I never truly doubt the connection, or at least not for long. I could go on for hours, because the ways some experiences happened are quite complex, but I won't. I'll just give you a few. In one, we helped a church in our presbytery, Trinity Presbyterian Church in Butler, Pennsylvania, recover from a pastoral calamity where their membership dropped from two hundred to seventeen in over four years. Seventeen! Think about that.

While we were helping them, it became clear they needed to rebuild the church's decaying front steps and porch. They got a bid for $35,000 to do that, as well as to install new doors and replace wood panels with glass ones around the door. It would significantly drain their savings. But they prayed, heard a call to do it, and pursued it with a genuine trust in God. I was so impressed with their faith. The week the bill came in, they received a check in the mail from the estate of a man who had died something like ten years before in the amount of $38,000.

At Calvin Presbyterian Church, we had a situation where we had grown to the point of needing to hire a part-time retired pastor to do pastoral care, and it would cost us $10,000. In our budgeting, we could only be confident of funding $6,000. Our board believed we were called to do it, even if we didn't have all the funds. So they voted to go forward with a belief the money would come. After our Christmas Eve service a week later, a woman who wasn't a member, but who regularly attended our church, approached me. She was one of a group of four women from a local retirement community who was attending our church. They never became members because they still wanted to be buried in their home churches. She said to me, "Pastor Graham, I want to tell you how much the other ladies and I love being in this church. You know we can't join because we want to be buried in our old churches' cemeteries, but we're still committed to this church. So we pooled our resources to make an end-of-year contribution." With that, she handed me a check for $4,000.

We've also had that happen here at Samaritan. We had a situation where I called a pastor about potentially establishing a satellite office in the church where he served. When we met, he told me he couldn't believe I was calling because he had already been thinking about calling me and asking me if we would be interested in putting a satellite office in his church. It's now there, and it's one of our fastest-growing offices.

Dawn: Wow! This is both really exciting and really scary. I want to believe in this, but . . .

Graham: You're still worried about what happens if God doesn't respond.

Dawn: Yes.

Graham: The only answer is to try. I think I'm quite scientific about this. Run an experiment in discernment and faith. Don't just think about it; actually try to do it the best you can by *literally* putting your trust in God. But you have to try it for a while. If you want to teach your church to do this, you have to lead them by doing it yourself. The key thing to remember is our emotions, especially our anxiety, can hijack our spirituality and hold our spirits hostage.

Dawn: So my spiritual battle is to allow my spirit to be stronger than my anxiety.

Graham: Yes, which—

Dawn: No more! How are we on time? I don't think my head can take more.

Graham: Sorry, I get very passionate about this, especially since it's a topic I'm reluctant to share with most people because they doubt the divine coincidences that arise from a deeper spiritual life. Many pastors who want their churches and themselves to be more spiritual have a hard time with these ideas because they don't seem rational enough. They get caught between the theological and the spiritual realm. One is rational. The other is experiential. What happens when the experience doesn't correspond to the rational?

These pastors will talk about discernment and even set up elaborate processes of discernment. What they're doing is creating a functional spirituality, where what matters is the process of discernment rather than discernment itself. I see this all over the place. So many denominations have incorporated the language of discernment into their decision-making, but they're just doing the same decision-making and calling it discernment. They may create more time for prayer; but because they haven't cultivated a culture of discernment where people expect to hear God, they're just dressing up functional decision-making in spiritual clothing. So, they immerse people in the techniques of discernment. But does that mean people are discerning?

Dawn: Yes, and that's what I'm having to grapple with now—how to shift from wanting a technique for discernment to creating a culture and lifestyle of discernment.

Graham: Let me give you the last word by asking you a final question before we end. What gets in the way of your becoming more open to this 3-D way of thinking about discernment?

Dawn: Yeah, I've been thinking about that. What gets in the way? I think you already defined it. It's my anxiety; but even more, it's my need to be in control of all of this. What you're talking about means both being in control and giving up control at the same time.

Graham: It's a paradox.

Dawn: Yes, it is, and it's really hard to do both at the same time. It's also doing things I've been on the edge of doing but I've been scared to do. This goes against all my training. I've been in a tradition that says we have to do everything "decently and in order." What you're talking about is doing everything decently and in order while also doing it uncertainly and "relinquishingly," if that's a word. It's saying we need to set up groups and processes and classes and retreats and stuff like that, while also letting God take care of it all. It's doing things and giving it all to God at the same time.

Graham: You're really nailing how it works. It's doing our part and letting God do God's part—trusting in that and not taking it back. I'm going to copy this one other quote from Hannah Whitall Smith:

> You have trusted Him in a few things, and He has not failed you. Trust Him now for everything, and see if He does not do for you exceedingly abundantly, above all that you could ever have asked or even thought, not according to your power or capacity, but according to His own mighty power, working in you all the good pleasure of His most blessed will.[7]

In other words, do your work and give the results to God, and trust in what God will do.

Dawn: Yeah. This really goes against my training.

Graham: Well, that's why we'll take our time and work on this.

Dawn: Good. I think I could talk for hours about this. My head is swirling with all sorts of ideas. But I also think I need to stop so I can let it settle.

Graham: I'm ready to stop. Let's pray.

FURTHER THOUGHTS

In my work as a spiritual director and clergy coach, what we explored throughout this chapter is both the hardest topic to delve into and the one I've often been the most reticent to discuss. It seems too fantastic. It doesn't seem rational. And as many times I've talked about it, I've mostly received puzzled looks and skeptical, cynical responses. Despite the fact the Gospels and Acts are filled with guidance on living this deeply connected, providential life with God, we're scared of it. I often wonder if that's why my tradition, the Presbyterian tradition, often talks about how much theology matters. Theology's important, but often it also becomes a haven for people who are scared of spiritual experience. I was reminded of this years ago when we had a large denominational meeting for pastors and elders at our church. We had an outdoor labyrinth, and we gave anyone interested an introduction to the labyrinth. One of the pastors approached me afterward and said, "Graham, I'm so fascinated with this labyrinth. I really wanted to join your introduction, but I had a big report to give later and was really worried I might have some sort of spiritual experience that would mess up my report."

The fact remains there is an incredibly strong strain within the Christian spiritual tradition that is grounded in an abandonment to God and a trust in divine providence. Episcopal laywoman Agnes Sanford wonderfully captured the basic theology of this approach when she wrote about her experiences in healing prayer:

> God is both within us and without us. He is the source of all life; the creator of universe behind universe; and of unimaginable depths of inter-stellar space and of light-years without end. But He is also the indwelling life of our own little selves. And just as a whole world full of electricity will not light a house unless the house itself is prepared to receive that electricity, so the infinite and eternal life of God cannot help us unless we are prepared to receive that light within ourselves. *Only the amount of God that we can get in us will work for us.*[8]

Many Christians might dismiss Sanford's beliefs as magical thinking or irrational wishing. Sanford's not alone in these beliefs, though. Others have written about their experiences of God's providential involvement. The Anglican mystic Evelyn Underhill writes:

A real man or woman of prayer, then, should be a live wire, a link between God's grace and the world that needs it. In so far as you have given your lives to God, you have offered yourselves, without conditions, as transmitters of His saving and enabling love: and the will and love, the emotional drive, which you thus consecrate to God's purposes, can do actual work on supernatural levels for those for whom you are called upon to pray. One human spirit can, by its prayer and love, touch and change another human spirit; it can take a soul and lift it to the atmosphere of God.[9]

These are people who have experienced this divine providence in their lives; and the more they've abandoned themselves to God, the more they've experienced these providences. One of the clearest writers on this was a missionary to the Philippines, Frank Laubach, who ran a radical experiment on living moment-by-moment with God (reflecting earlier writings of this commitment by the anonymous writer of *The Way of a Pilgrim* and Brother Lawrence of the Resurrection in his book *The Practice of the Presence of God*). Laubach was committed to turning his whole life into a prayer, trying to live in awareness and abandonment to God in every moment. As he did that, he began to experience a life of constant providence:

I feel simply carried along each hour, doing my part in a plan which is far beyond myself. This sense of cooperation with God in little things is what so astonishes me, for I never have felt this way before. I need something, and turn round to find it waiting for me. I must work, to be sure, but there is God working along with me. God takes care of all the rest. My part is to live this hour in continuous inner conversation with God and in perfect responsiveness to his will, to make this hour gloriously rich.[10]

Ultimately, this is a part of the Christian tradition that strives more for partnership with God in ministry rather than mere service. It recognizes while we are serving God as pastors, there's more there than just being stewards on God's behalf. We become leaders of congregations where God's presence, spirit, and grace begin to flow naturally because we are leading them to become open to this flow. And we lead them in this because the way of abandonment and providence has become more and more a part of our lives.

Normally at this point in a chapter I offer an exercise, but there isn't one that can prepare us for this way of ministry. Still, there are resources we can read to open ourselves up to it. So, the following bibliography may help, which is accompanied by a guide to reading the resources spiritually so they can become part of our prayer lives.

Spiritual Bibliography of Works Exploring God's Tangible Providence

Andreyevich Streltzoff, Piotr. *Father Arseny, 1893–1973: Priest, Prisoner, Spiritual Father*. Translated by Vera Bouteneff. Crestwood, NY: St. Vladimir's Seminary Press, 1998.

Anonymous. *The Way of a Pilgrim* and *The Pilgrim Continues His Way*. Translated by R. M. French. New York: HarperOne, 2010.

ten Boom, Corrie, and Elizabeth & John Sherrill. *The Hiding Place*. Grand Rapids, MI: Chosen Books, 2006.

de Caussade, Jean-Pierre. *The Sacrament of the Present Moment*. Translated by Kitty Muggeridge. San Francisco: HarperSanFrancisco, 2009.

Kelly, Thomas R. *A Testament of Devotion*. San Francisco: HarperSanFrancisco, 1992.

à Kempis, Thomas. *The Imitation of Christ*. Translated by William C. Creasy. Notre Dame, IN: Ave Maria Press, 1989.

Manning, Brennan. *Ruthless Trust: The Ragamuffin's Path to God*. San Francisco: HarperSanFrancisco, 2000.

Marshall, Catherine. *Beyond Ourselves: A Woman's Pilgrimage in Faith*. New York: McGraw Hill, 1961.

Sanford, Agnes. *The Healing Light.* New York: Ballantine Books, 1983.

Standish, N. Graham. *Discovering the Narrow Path: A Guide to Spiritual Balance.* Louisville, KY: Westminster John Knox Press, 2002.

Steindl-Rast, David. *Gratefulness, the Heart of Prayer: An Approach to Life in Fullness.* Ramsey, NJ: Paulist Press, 1984.

Underhill, Evelyn. *Life as Prayer.* New York: Morehouse Publishing, 1991.

Whitall Smith, Hannah. *The Christian's Secret of a Happy Life.* Grand Rapids, MI: Revell, 1952.

A GUIDE TO SPIRITUAL READING

WHAT IS SPIRITUAL READING?

Whether you actively sense it or not, God continually calls you to deepen your faith through prayer. God's spirit constantly nudges you to open your heart to God's wisdom, love, and grace. God regularly speaks, telling you how to live a deeper and better life. Unfortunately, life is so noisy that it's hard to distinguish God's voice from everything else. The practice of *spiritually* reading the Bible and the writings of great spiritual writers will help you discern God's voice more fully and clearly in your life.

HOW DO WE READ SPIRITUALLY AND PRAYERFULLY?

When we think of prayer, we normally think it's something we do in silence as we tell God about our concerns. This is one form of prayer, but our reading and thinking can also become prayer. Typically, we don't think of reading as prayer because we are used to analytical, critical, or recreational reading, not *spiritual* reading. Those kinds of readings lead us to read fast so we can understand what the book and the author say quickly. Spiritual reading is prayerful reading in which we read slowly and reflectively, trying to listen for what

God is saying to us through the book. This requires us to take our time and listen while we read.

We've been trained to read with our heads to "figure out" what we've read. We spend so much time trying to understand it intellectually that we generally miss what God may be saying to our heads *and* hearts. Spiritual reading invites us to read with both, asking, "What is God saying to me about my life? About God? About my calling?" Through spiritual reading, God slowly answers these questions.

The following steps can help turn your reading into a prayer discipline:

- Set aside a certain time, between twenty and thirty minutes, in a quiet place free of distractions for prayer and reading.
- Center yourself in a minute of silence.
- Ask God to speak to you and guide you through the reading.
- Read slowly and reflectively, ready to grapple with the reading with both your head and heart.
- Pause, reflect, and pray as you read. At times, you may have to put the book down to ponder what God is saying to you.
- If you disagree or don't understand something, ask God to help you. Resist the urge to be critical of the reading, which is how we are normally trained to read.
- At the end of each period of reading, offer your concerns to God in prayer, close in silence, and thank God for guiding you.

ELEMENTS OF SPIRITUAL READING

The following are other tips to help you grow spiritually through your readings:

- *Read Humbly.* Put aside your ego, biases, and expectations. Put aside your set theology so you can be open to how God may be challenging you. Let go of the need to agree or disagree with what you've read. Remember that at first, we often resist the truths God wants to reveal to us. There will be times when you won't like what you've read. Attend to what you sense God is saying rather than to what bothers you.

- *Read and Reread.* Spiritual reading involves dwelling, reflecting, and praying so we can discover deeper messages. Be willing to keep going over the same material.
- *Stress Quality Instead of Quantity.* Don't read material just to "get it done." Dwell on it, asking:
    - What is the basic message of God in this passage?
    - How does this message impact my life?
    - How do I apply what I am hearing to my life?
- *Stress Inspiration over Intellectual Insight or Emotional Impressions.* When we read intellectually, we can become overly critical or analytical. When we read emotionally, we often accept only those ideas that "feel right." Read from a place of receptivity that allows you to let go of your cherished beliefs and set opinions.
- *Be Patient and Trusting.* Stay with the passage even if you don't get any great ideas or insights, and especially if you don't understand it. Trust that God is speaking through the words you are reading. Sometimes, God speaks in very subtle ways. Patience gives subtle messages space to grow.
- *Wait for God to Disclose God's Mysteries.* God always works and speaks in mysterious ways because God inhabits the realm of the eternal. God is more patient and gentle than we are. So while you may get "aha!" moments, more often you'll get "hmmm" moments.
- *Remember, Spiritual Reading Is Reflective Reading.* To read spiritually means to read in a way that encourages repeated reflection of insights to gain even more inspirations. God won't just speak once, but God will speak many times through the same sentences or ideas. Great spiritual books can be read numerous times with new discoveries being made each time.

NOTES

1. Anthony de Mello, *Awareness: A de Mello Spirituality Conference in His Own Words* (New York: Doubleday, 1990).

2. Thomas Merton, *Thoughts in Solitude* (New York: Farrar, Straus, and Giroux, 1999), 47.

3. N. Graham Standish, "Leading a Church to Listen," in *Becoming a Blessed Church: Forming a Church of Spiritual Purpose, Presence, and Power* (Lanham, MD: Rowman & Littlefield, 2016), 143–66.

4. John 15:5.

5. Hannah Whitall Smith, *The Christian's Secret of a Happy Life* (Grand Rapids, MI: Revell, 1952), 193–94.

6. The actual quote is reportedly as follows: "When I pray, coincidences happen; when I don't, they don't." David Watson, *Called & Committed: World-Changing Discipleship* (Wheaton, IL: Harold Shaw Publishers, 1982), 83.

7. Whitall Smith, *The Christian's Secret of a Happy Life*, 72.

8. Agnes Sanford, *The Healing Light* (New York: Ballantine Books, 1983), 3. Emphasis in the original.

9. Evelyn Underhill, *Life as Prayer* (New York: Morehouse Publishing, 1991), 55.

10. Brother Lawrence and Frank Laubach, *Practicing His Presence* (Sargent, GA: The SeedSowers, 1973), 5.

TRANSFORMATIONAL PREACHING AND TEACHING

Ben is a solo pastor of a midsize Mennonite church in Northwestern Penn-sylvania. The church is in a large town near the border with Ohio. The area has a significant population of both Mennonite and Amish residents. He has been their pastor for three years.

The church is slightly conservative, sometimes mixing conservative poli-tics with religious beliefs, yet it is also committed to a variety of social justice issues. They care deeply about serving poor and single-parent families, as well as issues related to equality and integration, despite living in an area that is 98 percent white.

At the same time, they mix tenets of Christian faith with ideals of Amer-ican patriotism, which frustrates Ben. It's not that he's against patriotism. As he says, "It's that they believe God is really an American God." He wants to confront their political ideology at times but knows if he does, there will be a significant backlash. He also believes his church is losing its core sense of faith as it mimics the anxieties of the present age. He's tried to be tolerant of their mixing faith with politics, but it's led him to be somewhat obsessed with how superficial they've become and how they've become less and less Mennonite over time, which is a tradition that has often focused on being both biblically based and socially transformative.

In our previous three sessions, we discussed how to help the church over-come its resistance to a more gospel-oriented approach that calls into ques-

tion the alignment of one country's politics and Christian faith. We discussed the nature of resistance to change in a way similar to how it was discussed in chapter 3.

****

Graham: So . . . how's the resistance coming along?

Ben: You mean my struggle with their resistance? It's been giving me a lot to think about and even more questions. So, much of what we talked about last time in overcoming resistance—the need to be aware of where people are in their faith and their feelings, helping them feel safe when confronted with challenging ideas, and keeping my relationships with them in mind—is now making me question all the ways I'm dealing with them.

Graham: Has that been a bad thing?

Ben: No . . . it's just that it's gone against how I was trained. I was trained to believe if my biblical exegesis and explication are good, and if I give the congregation sound, rational arguments, they'll change. I'm realizing this approach hasn't been working.

I'm really struggling with where the church is right now. Our culture's anxiety seems to be infecting the whole soul of our church. It's like everyone's anxious about everything, and it's causing everyone to nitpick against each other.

Graham: I think I know what you mean, but give me an example.

Ben: Sure. We had a meeting the other night to talk about fixing steps that had been clipped when a truck hit them. It was like everyone hated everyone else's ideas. I had to stop the meeting and ask everyone to take a break before we could continue. They calmed down afterward, but that's a microcosm of our church.

Graham: So, it feels like the church is anxious?

Ben: Yeah. It also feels like it's becoming more superficial. No one seems to care as much about Christian theology. All they care about is cultural theology.

Graham: You mean their mixing of patriotism and Christianity that you talked about last time?

Ben: That . . . but also so much more. What do you do when it seems like the pull of the culture is so much stronger than the call of Christ?

Graham: I reach for Richard Foster.

Ben: Who?

Graham: Richard Foster. He wrote a great book on spiritual disciplines years ago, and he had this wonderful quote. (reaches for the book off a shelf and opens it) It's right here. I have the page marked because I refer to it often. Here's what he says:

> Superficiality is the curse of our age. The doctrine of instant satisfaction is a primary spiritual problem. The desperate need today is not for a greater number of intelligent people, or gifted people, but for deep people.[1]

I hold onto that quote, written in 1978, mind you, because it captures perfectly the struggle of the modern Christian faith, especially for those of us tasked with nurturing Christian faith. The struggle of any age for Christian pastors and teachers is to encourage people to become deeper people, especially in response to times of emotional turmoil.

Ben: It's gotten much worse than it was in 1978. Of course, what do I know? I was just a baby then.

Graham: Yeah, but there's good news in things getting worse. In many ways, our times have become very much like Jesus's times. Like then, we live in a time of competing philosophies and theologies in a world consumed with satisfying desires and urges, obsessed with ruthlessly achieving ambitions, and engaged in constant tribal conflict. Just as it was in the Roman Empire, our dominant culture has become shallow, conflicted, and self-consumed.

Ben: Do you really think our times are like Jesus's times?

Graham: I do. And I think the way out for us is to do what the early Christians did, which is to quit competing in the marketplace of ideas and to start competing in the marketplace of experience.

Ben: Okay, that sounds profound. What the heck does that mean?

Graham: (laughs) It's something I say a lot whenever people wonder why so many people have walked away from Christianity and the Christian faith. No one is wandering around saying, "Please, please teach me Mennonite theology. Please, please teach me Presbyterian beliefs." No one is asking for what we *believe*.

So many people now identify themselves as "spiritual, but not religious." When they do, they're criticizing us by saying we're "religious, but not spiritual." And they're right. They're telling us that the one thing they aren't looking for is our theology. They are searching for experience—the experience *of* God, not teachings, dogmas, doctrines, and orthodoxies *about* God. By the way, whenever I say this to pastors, they feel like they have to defend theology. I'm not saying we need to get rid of theological thinking. I'm simply saying our overemphasis on theology often minimizes the pursuit of spiritual experiences, and people are seeking the experiences. In my whole life as a pastor, no one has ever come up to me and said, "Please teach me Presbyterian theology!" They have asked me many times to teach them how to find God.

When we emphasize logical, rational theological teaching and preaching, people tune us out because they don't see Christian beliefs as rational or logical. And they're right. Whether we admit it or not, many of our beliefs don't make logical sense. How can God be one and three at the same time? How can God be born of a virgin, die, and be resurrected by God who is dead? Why does Jesus teach that to be strong, we have to be weak; to be rich, we have to be poor; to live, we have to die; to gain our lives, we must lose our lives; to be mature, we must become like children? These don't make logical sense. I even wrote a book about how engaging with these paradoxes leads us to a realm beyond logic and into the realm of experiencing God.[2] The problem is we keep trying to reach out to people by making our beliefs seem rational and logical. They know they're not.

So, what are they all seeking? They're seeking *experience*. And those experiences aren't just intellectual experiences. They're emotional, physical, and relational. They want to experience the divine, the holy, the supernatural. They want an experience of God that both transforms their lives and gives them a greater sense of peace, understanding, purpose, and meaning. When we help them experience God, then they're willing to grapple with the often-paradoxical teachings of Christianity and appreciate them as profound spiritual insights. But as long as we try to make everything about logic and rationality, we lose. That doesn't mean we abandon logic. It means we emphasize the connection with God that leads to something deeper.

Ben: This gets back to the emotional stuff you talked about last time, when you said we can't reach people if we're also not reaching them at an emotional level.

Graham: Yes, it also gets back to another little phrase I've often used both for myself and in training seminary interns: "No one becomes a Christian because it makes rational sense. They become Christian because they've experienced God."

Ben: So, how does this all relate to their mixing politics and religion?

Graham: Sorry . . . What makes it easy for church members to mix their political and religious beliefs is that the two are equivalent in their minds. In fact, many people have had deeper experiences of community and something transcendent through their patriotism than through their church. Perhaps they've served in the military. Perhaps they've attended Fourth of July and Memorial Day parades. They may have supported the country through three, four, five, or more wars. They're probably somewhat involved politically; and as they watch cable news each night, they emotionally connect with people who share their political beliefs. And cable news knows that. They know how to appeal to people on an emotional level that masquerades as a logical level by encasing their arguments in a veneer of rationality. What makes people more passionate about their politics than their theology is politics is all about experience. Is church about experience?

Ben: No, not really, although shouldn't they feel some sort of experience by going to church every Sunday?

Graham: Perhaps, but what is that experience? Their experiences of the culture evoke passion. What do our worship services evoke? Do we evoke passion? Do we evoke a deep sense of peace? Do we evoke a deep sense of connection with God?

Ben: This is opening a whole can of worms because I know all this, yet I can't change our worship services and make them like parades. And I certainly can't make them become like going to war.

Graham: Nope. But there are things you can do.

Ben: Like what?

Graham: Like making sure your preaching and teaching are *transformative* rather than *informative*.

Ben: What?

Graham: Transformative rather than informative.

Ben: I get the "transformative" part, but what do you mean by "informative"?

Graham: I apologize, because I can't explain it simply without doing a bit of teaching. And I've already been talking a lot. Anyway, here goes. For me, the difference is rooted in an experience I had while studying spirituality as part of my doctorate. During my first two years of doctoral studies in spirituality, I took a three-semester "Spiritual Classics" course, which was a deep dive into the writings of the Christian spiritual masters throughout Christian history.

What truly transformed my thinking was *A Testament of Devotion*, a book by the Quaker writer Thomas Kelly.[3] It opened up a whole new way of understanding the spiritual life. But it wasn't just the book that impacted me. It was how we read it. I already knew how to read books in a typical, academic way—with an eye toward grasping the *information*. We read Kelly's book differently. We were trained to read it *formatively*, which led to my *transformation*. Reading formatively meant reading in a way that turns the reading into a prayerful dialogue with God.

We've all been trained to read *informatively*. Years of schooling have drilled us to read relatively quickly to get the information *into* us, so we can then regurgitate it on an exam or in a paper—or even a sermon. Years of reading news and gossip has similarly trained us to read quickly and informatively.

Formative reading (also called *spiritual reading*) is different. It's intentionally slow, prayerful, and reflective, allowing what we read to deeply shape our lives.[4] Kelly's book *transformed* me. His emphasis on God's presence within, on God's grace working around us everywhere, and on God actively creating a blessed, grace-filled core in every church captured my imagination, especially because it wasn't a typically Presbyterian brand of spirituality, which tends to be more intellectual and less incarnational. The practice of formative reading also helped me realize our churches had become overly *informative* rather than *formative*. It gave me insight into why so many people have walked away from Christianity: *they want spiritual formation and transformation, not just religious and theological information.*

We've been trained to preach and teach theological information *about* Christian beliefs in our sermons and classes. We teach the context and history around a passage. We tell people what the biblical characters did, said, and taught. We give people religious facts and history. All of this is important, but this *information* by itself often fails to deeply *transform* people's lives. It offers important information *about* God and life rather than connecting us experientially *with* God in a way that helps us live deeply spiritual, compassionate lives.

Learning to read formatively taught me how to pastor in a transformative way. It taught me that everything we do in a church has the power to shape and transform people spiritually, relationally, mentally, physically, and pragmatically. Everything from preaching to teaching to meetings to ministry to mission can nurture deeper spiritual lives that lead to deeper lives of service.

It helped me realize ministry and mission flow out of the spiritual life as we spiritually mature. In effect, our mainline Christian Protestant bias is we often think getting people to engage more in ministry and mission is about logically and rationally convincing them they should be more engaged. In other words, we think as we give them adequate information about what they should do, they'll do that. The Christian spiritual life approaches ministry and mission differently. It recognizes that ministry and mission are a deeply felt response to the experiences of God that lead us to want God's love to flow through our lives. It recognizes that as we grow spiritually, we naturally become more ministry- and mission-minded. We don't become navel-gazers. We become like the apostles as we form a passion for serving Christ.

Ben: Is this part of the Presbyterian tradition?

Graham: Actually, as I mentioned before, I'm digging deeper than Presbyterian, but to answer your question, not especially. It is very much a part of the Mennonite tradition. Your tradition is a transforming one in which Menno Simons walked away from the Roman Catholic priesthood because he had a passion for transforming lives, which he believed the Roman Catholic Church at the time wasn't doing. There is also a transforming nature to Presbyterianism, but in many ways, we haven't known what to do with it. So, we describe it as mere "piety," which makes it sound more emotional and sappy. Our tradition tends to be more intellectual and theological. Perhaps that's why we've shrunk faster than most other denominations. We're more out of step with a culture that wants something spiritual rather than just theological.

Ben: Okay, I see what you mean. We're not as theological as you all are. Simons focused on believers' baptism and making an adult choice because he wanted people to have the opportunity to make a transforming choice for God.

Graham: And I suppose it's also why he tended to use the Song of Solomon as his main metaphor for the church. It was his way of talking about how transforming love is all that matters—love that transforms us and others.

Ben: Right. How do you know about Mennonite tradition?

Graham: From working with a few Mennonites before you. I had to read about your tradition to keep up. Anyway, being transformative means leading people to become more deeply spiritual.

Ben: Okay, I get we're supposed to be transformative in our preaching and teaching. How do we do that?

Graham: Again, it's hard to give a simple answer. Let me take a stab at an example. Easter was only a month ago. What was the gist of your Easter sermon?

Ben: Do you want the whole thing or the short version?

Graham: Perhaps the short version would be better.

Ben: I talked about how important it was that Jesus died for our sins and how we can now live forgiven lives because of it. I talked about how hard it is for some people to believe in his resurrection and how it's okay because even the disciples didn't until they were given proof. I talked about how important it is for us to believe even when believing is hard. And I talked about how we can have confidence in this because John tells us he witnessed all of this. And then I told a story about a friend of mine who went to rehab, read John's Gospel while he was there, and had an epiphany that has helped him stay sober for the past five years.

Graham: What was the epiphany?

Ben: Um, that he was the branch of the vine Jesus mentioned in John 15. He realized that instead of being grafted to the vine and allowing grace to flow through him, he had previously been grafted to the bottle and mainly let the alcohol flow through him. That was why his life never bore any fruit.

Graham: Wow! So, listening to this, and realizing I'm not getting the whole sermon, it sounds like your sermon was mostly informational, *but* at the end, it became transformational. The sermon was informational when it focused on what happened 2,000 years ago. You gave historical "information" about Jesus's crucifixion. Then you gave theological "information" about his forgiving us. Then you tried to help them accept the historical "information" that he was resurrected. You used logic as a way of trying to convince them the resurrection was real.

My guess is your argument didn't sway the skeptics who were there because their family made them come to church. Where the important part comes in is at the end, when you told them how to personally connect with the resurrected Christ through your friend's story. You talked about an experience your friend had that gave something of a blueprint for people to be transformed. Let me ask you a question: after the sermon, which part of the sermon did people give you feedback on?

Ben: The story.

Graham: Yeah, not the other stuff, because they already knew that stuff. They've heard it every Easter of their lives. So, let me reshape that sermon in a more transformative way. What if you started by saying, "Today I'm going to tell you about the resurrection," and then told the story? And then used it as a metaphor where you talked about our relationship with Christ in the here and now, and how our main responsibility is remaining grafted to the vine? What if you talked about the gift of Jesus's resurrection as meaning we are always able to connect with Christ in a personal, transforming way? And what if you told them they didn't have to believe in the resurrection to experience the resurrected Christ? They can experience him for themselves by opening themselves up to Christ and asking him to enter their lives. And what if you finished by telling one or two shorter stories of people experiencing their own resurrection by being connected with Christ?

Ben: I don't know if I have that many stories.

Graham: Yeah, I get that. But part of our not having stories is we don't look for transforming stories. In fact, I think many of us in the mainline Protestant churches feel uncomfortable using transforming stories. They don't feel intellectual enough.

Ben: That may be me. I was actually a little scared to tell the story about my friend. I was worried people would think I'm too much like Joel Osteen.

Graham: (laughs) Why is becoming too much like Joel Osteen every mainline Protestant pastor's fear? You're not alone. I discovered years ago how averse pastors are to transforming stories. I was the spiritual director for an Episcopal priest. I believe she's a bishop now. Anyway, I was telling her I often used stories from one of the *Chicken Soup for the Soul* books, and sometimes from *Guideposts Magazine*, before it got so focused on celebrities.

She was aghast. "You're a smart man. How can you use those stories?"

"Now that I have three masters and a PhD, I'm free to use whatever I want. I don't have to prove my intellectual cred," I said. The point wasn't that I was smart. It was that I no longer had to prove my academic "cred" and I am free to engage people experientially where they are.

My point was, as much as we may dislike Joel Osteen, and as shallow as we may think he is, his sermons are roughly 80 percent transformation and 20 percent information. I believe ours are the inverse, and perhaps even 90 percent information. Even if we were able to get to 50/50 in our formation/information ratio, it would make a difference.

Ben: Yeah, this is throwing me for a loop because I'm now realizing my whole style is informational. And I'm realizing trying to do what you're saying feels like a betrayal of all I've been taught through my seminary training. I was taught to be intellectual and informational. I was taught to spend the bulk of my time exploring the historical and social context of the passage. Connecting with the emotional and transformational feels manipulative.

Graham: I hear you. It took me a long time to permit myself to do this.

Ben: How did you give yourself permission?

Graham: I had an epiphany twenty-five years ago. I realized each time I preached, I was preaching for my seminary professors and peers, and they weren't there. I then realized the glazed looks I was getting were because I wasn't helping people get involved in my sermons. I wasn't inviting them in. I was giving wonderfully intellectual sermons for people who wanted pragmatic, transformational help for living their lives. I realized they were experiencing 80 percent of their lives at the emotional and intuitive levels, not the intellectual level. I'll never be the kind of preacher who elicits tears or anything like that; but I realized if I wanted to help them transform their lives, I had to change how I preached. So, I started watching those "off-limits" preachers, teachers, and motivational speakers who were better at actually transforming lives, and I adopted elements from their speaking.

Ben: Like Joel Osteen?

Graham: No, not him specifically. He came along long after I graduated from seminary. But I've watched him and understand how he preaches, although I have no interest in imitating him. It's a good exercise to study him, but you have to watch and listen from a stance where you're ready to learn, not from a cynical, critical stance.

Ben: Okay, so if you were going to give me the short version of transformative preaching principles, what would they be?

Graham: Putting me on the spot! I've not necessarily written these down, but I'll try to give you ideas. I think it starts with beginning your preparation with a few questions: "What is the simple message God is calling me to preach that will help transform their lives?" This question means you have to start your sermon prep in prayer.

Then you ask, "How has my life been shaped by this message, or how does it reflect how my life has been transformed?"

Finally, ask, "How can I share this with them in a way that will be transforming for them?" With this last question, you have to reflect on where people are emotionally and spiritually so you can connect with them. If you believe they're somewhat emotionally and spiritually resistant, you start there. Start where you think most are.

The key is you start with transformation, not exegesis. Exegesis can be useful, but it has to serve transformation. It has to supply information that supports transformation and reformation. If you start with exegesis and make it all about who, where, what, when, why, then it gives them information that leads nowhere.

Ben: If I'm hearing you right, you're not saying to do away with the information. You're saying the information has to serve transformation. In other words, if all that background to a passage doesn't help change people's lives, it isn't helpful. But if it can help change people's lives, use it.

Graham: Right! So, that's the first thing—*start with focusing on messages that are transforming.* A second thing I've learned is to *always make the message simple, even if it's complex.* I don't mean simplistic. I mean make the main idea something people can capture relatively easily, which makes it harder for you to put together. This is hard because we tend to love intellectual complexity. It's more interesting to us. But whenever we create a complex sermon, we lose people. A way of thinking about this is by asking what ideas or concepts have shaped your life. Have they been the long, complex ideas you listened to over a long period, or were they short statements that opened you up?

Over the years, I've read many complex things, but it's the short, simple statements that have made a difference in my life. For instance, years ago I was transformed by something William Temple, the Archbishop of Canterbury in the 1940s, said: "When I pray, coincidences happen; when I don't, they don't." Or something a colleague said to me a few weeks ago: "Holding onto resentment is like drinking poison and then waiting for the other person to die." Another simple phrase that taught me how to navigate through the tensions of life came from Thomas Kelly, whom I mentioned before: "Ponder this paradox in religious experience: 'Nothing matters; everything matters.'"[5] Crafting complex ideas into simple statements allows them to sink in and stick with us. If you can't summarize your sermon's main idea in one simple sentence, then it may be too complex and more suitable for two sermons.

Another idea is *to craft your sermon to be said, not read*. People are listening to the sermon, not reading it, which means they can't go back and reflect on something you just said. If your sermon's too complex, you'll end up taking them down rabbit holes that cause them to lose focus on your words. This is related to simplicity, but it's more than that. It means crafting what you say in a way that flows naturally. It also means getting rid of religious jargon. The way I often say it to seminary interns I've worked with is to make your point as you would to someone sitting across a restaurant table from you. Make it conversational. Make it simple. So, don't say, "We need to celebrate the fact we are all dwelling in the kingdom." Say, "When I feel God's presence all around me, I can't help but feel joyful." The key is your sermons are verbal dialogue, not grad school papers.

Ben: Right, I think I keep my sermons simple, but I hadn't thought of also crafting simple statements. This is really hard, though, because it's easy to get caught up in the complex thoughts. And I haven't truly thought about saying things to be said, not read.

Graham: And you were trained in seminary to think, write, and speak abstractly, and to express complex thoughts compositionally rather than verbally. Your main tasks in seminary were reading complex books and then writing complex papers that professors, trained in complex thinking, have a whole week to read as they sift through students' attempts at expressing complex thoughts. Meanwhile, on Sundays, you have twenty to thirty minutes to get a point across, and they won't get to go back and reread what you said. It's one shot. If they space out, which many do when sermons get complex, you never get them back. Therefore, you lose the sermon's transformative power. What most of us don't appreciate is how we've been transformed when someone has said something complex in an amazingly simple way. In fact, this is what separates true geniuses from us. They know how to take amazingly complex ideas and distill them down into incredibly simple phrases.

Ben: Yeah, I'm tracking you there—both on the genius stuff and the need to simplify things. I have one guy, Sam, who falls asleep during every single one of my sermons. I've been blaming him, thinking he's either lazy or just needs to get a CPAP machine.[6] Maybe the problem is that I've been too complex.

Graham: You'll also notice others start to shift around in their seats. Having a simple, but profound, idea at the center of your sermon gets them leaning in, especially if it applies to their lives and reflects their struggles. I had someone like your Sam. I made it my mission to keep him awake!

Ben: Copy that! Other ideas?

Graham: Yeah . . . Unfortunately, you've asked me to share my ideas on preaching, and I've been storing up these ideas for a long time. I get to teach in conferences, retreats, seminars, and classes about many subjects but rarely about preaching, even though I've thought about it often. My ideas have developed from the fact I've always been a bit of an ADD[7] iconoclast who's sensitive to what causes people to tune out.

Ben: That's okay. That's why I'm here.

Graham: Okay. I have a few others. We can keep exploring this down the road, but these are things I think are essential. Another idea I have is *for sermons to be transformative, they need to speak across multiple intelligences*, and we've tended to apply sermons mostly to one set of intelligence—intellectual intelligence.

I don't know if you've ever heard of Howard Gardner. He's a Harvard researcher who's studied how we all have different kinds of intelligences beyond intellectual and how our culture's obsession with intellectual intelligence has stunted us.[8] He has identified several intelligences, although they've shifted over the years, depending on in which book you find the list.[9]

You can look them up later online, but there are a few that are really important for preaching. We already understand the *verbal-lin-guistic intelligence*, which has to do with language and crafting how something is both read and said.

We also somewhat understand Gardner's *logical-mathematical intelligence*, which has to do with crafting everything according to a rational, logical scheme. That's part of the theological yearning every denomination and tradition has, and it's mostly what IQ tests measure.

Put those aside for now. Another crucially important one is *interpersonal intelligence,* which is understanding relationships. If your sermon isn't relational, then it will miss those who are intelligent about relationships.

Ben: How the heck do you make sermons interpersonally intelligent?

Graham: Oh, it has to do with whether you look at people while talking, whether you stand behind a pulpit or walk about among them. If you craft your sentences more conversationally, like what we talked about a few minutes ago.

Ben: Right. Table. Restaurant . . . like a date.

Graham: Yeah. Don't bore your date with technical, intellectual, theological stuff. You'll never get a second date.

Ben: Preaching as dating. That's a really weird concept.

Graham: It is, but I always found it helpful too. Anyway, another is *intrapersonal intelligence*. That's the ability of people to be self-reflective. This is where the simply crafted, profound statements come in. If you make a simple statement that resonates, people will reflect on it. Stories are also part of this kind of intelligence, although they cross intelligences and actually bind several together. Stories lead to self-reflection because the transformative ones draw us into them. Stories that really capture people are those where people go through some sort of struggle and are changed in the end because of their spiritual experience of God in some way.

Another intelligence is what he calls *existential intelligence*. That's essentially spiritual or transcendent intelligence; but being a psychologist, Gardner had to find a more scientific word for it—not that scientists readily accept the word "existential." Anyway, sermons need to speak to the spiritual, the transcendent, the beyond. They need to speak about things we can't see, hear, touch, taste, or feel, while using all of those senses metaphorically. In effect, if your sermon is overly theological and lacking in the spiritual, you miss people.

Ben: So, what would you say the big difference between theology and spirituality is?

Graham: Theology is more intellectual and ascribes to logical-mathematical intelligence. It is trying to create a system for understanding the spiritual so it makes logical sense. The spiritual is more experiential. Theology thinks *about* God. Spirituality engages us *with* God. It is really important to have theological concepts and constructs that help us think about God, the meaning of life, creation, and all matters in heaven and on earth. But theological reflection isn't a substitute for transforming experiences. Unfortunately, we often substitute theological thinking for spiritual experience in the mainline Protestant church.

Ben: Okay, my head is spinning at this point. Do you remember how earlier you said preachers need to make sermons simple, and crafting simple sentences is important?

Graham: Yeah?

Ben: Can you do that with this?

Graham: Yes! (laughs) I guess I'm guilty of not practicing what I preach. Okay, here goes. Ultimately to preach transformationally, you need to preach a relatively simple, but not simplistic, message you repeat across intelligences. So, you share your thoughts intellectually. But then you share the same message through a story. Then you share it again through some sort of symbol, object lesson, piece of music, video clip, poem, or picture. You then give listeners something to reflect on by inviting them to think about a sentence, symbol, event, or something else.

The point is don't just try to preach in one way. Preach multiple ways. The more you integrate multiple intelligences while preaching the same, compelling idea, the more you preach to the full breadth of those who are listening and the full breadth of those who are seeking an experience of God throughout their lives.

170

So, I'm going to summarize by bringing up that dreaded name again—Joel Osteen. Why do we mainline Protestant church pastors dislike him so much? A huge part is because he doesn't appeal to our mainline Protestant, logical-mathematical intelligence. He is *not* very intellectual, and we value the intellectual. But he is masterful at integrating all the other intelligences. And he's preaching to people who have walked away from our churches. I believe we can be who we are and integrate more of what he does. We can be intellectual and speak across all of those other intelligences at the same time. That's how we become transformative.

Okay, you're now becoming like that guy who sleeps through your sermons. I can tell you're tired.

Ben: Yeah, but it's good. It's just a lot to think about. I do hear what you're saying, which is we need to bring together many different ways of speaking to people if we're going to get them to tune in and help them be transformed through our preaching. I assume you would say this applies to teaching too.

Graham: Yep. Maybe it's even more important in teaching because you generally teach longer, although students in a class are also usually willing to work harder to follow you.

Ben: I get that.

Graham: Can I indulge one more idea about transformative teaching and preaching with you?

Ben: Will it help me, and can you give it to me simply?

Graham: (laughs) I think yes to both.

Ben: Okay.

Graham: I am aware of all the energy I'm taking up, so I'll try to make this as easy as possible. I want to talk with you about *asymmetrical* preaching. This is an idea I developed years ago, and it's amazing how transforming it can be. Here goes: We've been trained to preach *symmetrically*. What I mean is whenever we want to talk about a topic, especially a controversial one that's likely to lead to resistance, we tend to preach about it in a direct, one-to-one way.

So, let's say we're going to talk about the need to love people who are homosexual. I realize you may have a different view than I do, but it's a good example because when we address this topic, we usually talk about it symmetrically. We'll start by telling the congregation we're going to talk about homosexuality. Then we make our case for or against it. We then pull out passages from the Bible that speak against it or support the need for people to be tolerant and accepting. Then we emphatically summarize our point, trying to motivate the congregation to change their minds if they disagree. No matter how well we craft our case, though, those who don't share our perspective aren't going to be transformed. Why not? Because people don't form their opinions on these topics intellectually. They form opinions from their experiences and how they "feel" about the topic, even if they say their opinions are based on a rational, faithful, theological reading of the Bible.

Ben: Right. That's my congregation. I don't have a problem with homosexuality, although the Pride parades bother me a little. My congregation, though, is all over the place. Many see homosexuals as immoral and get angry at those who disagree.

Graham: Yep. So, this is where asymmetry comes in. I'm pretty much where you are theologically. When we preach symmetrically on a topic, it allows people to build their counterpoints. In fact, once they figure out what your case is, they no longer listen to your points. They're consumed with finding the flaws in your points. They're formulating their arguments against you. They're reacting symmetrically to you. You make one case, and they formulate the opposite case.

For those who don't want to hear what you have to say, it actually puts them in a position of having to decide whether to stay and listen to you or get up and walk out.

Ben: I've had a few of those.

Graham: I haven't, but it's because I deal with topics like this asymmetrically. Asymmetrical means you come to the topic from a direction they don't expect. You don't confront it head-on. You confront it while teaching something else.

For example, back in 2002, I did a sermon on Matthew 25:31–46—the parable of the sheep and goats who are separated on Jesus's left and right. I talked about how important it was for us to care about people struggling on the margins. To them, I was talking about the poor, the hungry, the poorly clothed, those in prison, and all those described in the passage. I read a poem about six people around a fire, each with their own logs, and how they wouldn't throw their logs in because they didn't want them to provide heat for the people who weren't like them.[10] I talked about how easy it is for us to find some group, any group, that we don't like and how Christ calls us to love and embrace them anyway.

They were going along with me because who could argue against Christ's call to love people who are poor, imprisoned, hungry, homeless, and the like? Who could argue against loving those on the margins? I talked about all of those conditions and how our response is to contribute to the food bank and do clothing drives, how I have visited people in prison as have others, and the need to always look for ways to care about the marginalized. Then I closed by sharing an experience I had:

My wife, Diane, was a social worker who mainly worked with hemophiliacs infected by HIV contracted from the blood-clotting-factor injections they had to take regularly to keep from constant bleeding. As a result of her work, she became very involved in the AIDS community around Pittsburgh. She helped coordinate a yearly retreat called "The Healing Weekend." It was a men's retreat with entertainment, motivational speakers, and workshops for those with HIV/AIDS and their families, and many attending the retreats were gay.

One year, the Episcopal priest, who annually presided over a healing worship service near the end of the weekend, couldn't make it because he was sick. So, I agreed to conduct the service. I was a little nervous because I wasn't sure how they would accept me, a heterosexual pastor from a denomination that, at the time, didn't allow gay ordination or marriages, and that they experienced as hating them.

When it came time to offer the healing prayers, I had all of them gather in a circle around the altar (it was a Roman Catholic retreat center). I went around the circle, asking each person's name in turn, praying over each one, and anointing his forehead with oil in the shape of a cross. About every second or third man would weep as I prayed and anointed him.

Afterward, one of them approached me and asked, "Do you know why so many of the men were crying?"

"I imagine it was because I prayed for healing from AIDS," I said.

"No," he said. "It's because you're the first straight pastor to ever pray for them and touch them while doing so. They're used to being hated by all Christians. They're not used to having a straight pastor care about them."

Ben: Wow.

Graham: Yeah . . . wow. That experience has stuck with me. It's also asymmetrical. I wasn't preaching about homosexuality. I was preaching about compassion, love, and reaching out as Jesus taught in Matthew 25. Even if you are a conservative who believes homosexuality is wrong, what do you do with a story like that? It's still a story about love. Of course, someone might angrily assert I never should have prayed for them, but that person would have an extremely cold heart.

My sermon first got them thinking about love, compassion, and reaching out to those on the margins. Then I told a story about gay men on the margin. The story pushed people to look at themselves through the eyes of these men who had felt profoundly rejected. It was a transformative story. These kinds of stories, when told in a different context, reduce resistance. People can reject my theology on the subject, but they can't just say my experience didn't happen, nor can they say my experience didn't matter. The asymmetry is getting people thinking one way about a topic they agree with, and then introducing a tangent that pushes them to struggle with their cherished views. They may not ultimately agree with us, but they have to struggle with it.

Ben: I have to think about this for a while too.

Graham: And you've had enough.

Ben: And I've had enough.

Graham: I am sorry for dominating this so much. It's just that it's hard to introduce new concepts without going into detail.

Ben: No, I get it. Thanks.

FURTHER THOUGHTS

One of the things I notice that really afflicts us in the mainline Protestant church is how reluctant we are to move out of our intellectual comfort zones. As I mentioned in the preface, Gillian Tett, a former anthropologist turned *New York Times* business journalist, calls our tendency to build walls around our perspectives the "silo effect." I'll remind you what she said:

> People often live in separate mental and social "ghettos," talking and coexisting only with people like us. In many countries, politics is polarized. Professions seem increasingly specialized, partly because technology keeps becoming more complex and sophisticated, and is only understood by a tiny pool of experts.[11]

Her point is that we become fragmented as we interact and talk only with those who already agree with us. This becomes a problem if we are committed to helping people transform through our preaching and teaching. How? We tend to stay in our traditional silos, preaching only in ways we've seen and been taught to preach and teach. And let's be honest: fewer and fewer people are clamoring for this type of preaching and teaching. We may not like it, but they're ignoring us while they're listening to people like Joel Osteen, Oprah, Eckhart Tolle, Daniel Amen, Deepak Chopra, Andy Stanley, Brené Brown, Krista Tippett, or a hundred other people who aren't in the mainline Protestant church tradition.

It's not just them we ignore. For the most part, we in the mainline Protestant church world gravitate toward siloed theological concepts and ideas that frame our way of thinking. As a result, we stay in our own theological and denominational silos and don't pay attention to what is taking place in the fields of neuroscience, psychology, sociology, anthropology, business, marketing, organizational development, and so much more. We stay with what makes us comfortable, but that also renders us unable to communicate with people who are already stepping out of their silos and integrating ideas from so many different perspectives.

One of the hallmarks of the post-modern age is that people are no longer seeking that one, true perspective of reality. They are willing to look at life from many different angles. While they embrace several new ideas, they have become increasingly resistant to the mainline Protestant Christian perspective.

Preaching transformationally requires understanding transformation not only from our perspective, but also from a variety of others. What does recent brain research say about how prayer changes the brain? What is the impact of research on how the right and left brain hemispheres work together to help us understand and interact in the world? What does the marketing field tell us about effective communication? Many pastors see marketing as manipulative, but only manipulative marketing is manipulative. The rest is all about communicating effectively so ideas stick. What can we learn from psychology about mental illness, personality disorders, learning, loving, divorce, and growth and maturity? What can sociology and anthropology teach us about the way culture works?

As long as we stay in our silos, we become less and less effective in reaching out to people living in the real world. And this impacts our preaching. If our preaching is siloed, meaning it's only speaking to the already converted, it loses its ability to transform. At this point, it only has the power to retain those who already believe what we believe. Yet that power is diminishing because even those people, over time, will get out of their religious silos and embrace ideas we shun.

It's important to leave your silo and read something that will help make your preaching and teaching more formative and transformative. I invite you to read a book I wish I could put in every mainline Protestant church pastor's hands. The book is *Made to Stick* by Chip and Dan Heath.[12]

Chip Heath is a business professor at Stanford University. His brother, Dan, is an entrepreneur who teaches at Duke University's CASE Center.[13] Their book tells us why some messages stick with us decades later while most fade away almost instantly. They've come up with a relatively simple acronym for the six elements of a sticky message: SUCCESs.[14] They say that the most powerful, sticky messages are those that combine these six elements. Often when we preach or teach, we use only one or two of these elements, which makes our sermons and classes forgettable. As the exercise for this chapter, I invite you to read their book (after you finish this one, of course). What's amazing about these six elements is when we communicate in a way that integrates them as much as possible, we communicate across multiple intelligences:

- *Simple*—The Heaths highlight that the most powerful messages are the ones that capture profound ideas in simple ways, as we explored earlier in this chapter. This is what geniuses do. They explore complex ideas and then help others grasp them. Simple doesn't mean simplistic. Simple means easy to grasp quickly. These are ideas, such as John F. Kennedy's "Ask not what your country can do for you—ask what you can do for your country,"[15] or the Rolling Stones' "You can't always get what you want. But if you try sometimes you'll find you get what you need."[16] Simple can also be in the sermon's construction, making it about one idea, rather than multiple ideas, that you speak to intellectually, emotionally, and metaphorically.

- *Unexpected*—People crave surprise. You know this already, but you may not have attached this idea to your sermons. What makes music enjoyable is a surprising refrain, hook, or instrumental solo. What makes movies and television shows compelling is not knowing who did something until the end, and having lots of smaller, surprising possibilities in between. Much of mainline Protestant preaching lacks the unexpected. We preach in predictable ways—using the same format, the same kinds of stories, the same points repeatedly every week. In my preaching, I've often strived to bring something surprising into a sermon, whether it's a movie clip, a story, a twist to the way we think about something, an object, a dance, or a popular song. For example, I once preached on the topic of discernment and how to follow God, wanting to stress the idea that following God means letting things unfold. So when people came to worship that morning, we gave everyone a folded slip of paper that was taped shut and told them not to open it. At the appropriate time during the sermon, I asked the congregation to open them. The slip of paper said, "Trust God and let life unfold."

- *Concrete*—Often mainline Protestant pastors criticize nondenominational and Pentecostal preaching for its lack of depth. However, there's a reason for this style, and it's related to why so many of these churches grow and ours don't. These pastors are very good at making their sermons practical and applicable. Mainline Protestant pastors love to explore abstract ideas and ideals. We like to talk theologically and even poetically. The problem is people are seeking practical, concrete guidance on how to live their lives. Great communication finds ways to make lessons tangible. So instead of talking about how we are forgiven because of Christ's sacrifice on the cross, what if we talk about how being forgiven plays out in everyday life—how this can lead us to forgive people for the pain they have caused us? Instead of just talking about how God loves us, talk about how this love plays out in daily life—how we can live with the confidence that we aren't bad and how we can share that love with others? The key is figuring out how to use concrete stories to bring these ideas to life in people's lives.

- *Credible*—Making a sermon credible doesn't mean using lots of research statistics or even proving theologically that something in the Bible is true. Credibility is subjective to the listener. So we must help people *feel* what we're saying is true. There are many methods for doing this. Some involve how we tell stories. If our stories are general and abstract, they will lack credibility. For example, how credible does this story sound? "I met a person years ago who gave me a message from God about how loved I am." When stories include details we can connect with, they gain credibility. Contrast the first story with this one:

> I was at the Philadelphia train station three years ago, waiting for a train to New York. While I was standing there, I was also silently struggling with my life. I kept wondering, "Is it all worthwhile?" For a fleeting moment

> I thought about jumping in front of a train, but I couldn't do that to my family. As I was standing there, I dropped my ticket. A woman picked it up and gave it to me. She took a long look at my face and then said with a smile, "You do know God loves you deeply, don't you?" I started to get teary-eyed.

This second story is credible because of the details and the emotions of it. The key is that a sermon story gains credibility when it's told in a way that helps people feel they are witnessing the story firsthand.

- *Emotional*—People seek emotional connection more than intellectual connection. Every therapist knows this, but too few pastors practice this when they preach. To bring emotion into our preaching doesn't mean making it sappy. It does mean exploring emotions. Using the previous example, if we were giving a sermon on how God loves us, bring the emotional struggle into it:

  > We all know through the Bible, and sermons, and books that God loves us, but we don't always feel we are loved. So many people in life criticize us, ignore us, and reject us, and those experiences can leave us feeling constantly anxious, guilty, and sad. Discovering that God loves us often means grappling with these emotions. The answer isn't numbing ourselves. It is spending time in places where we can feel something different. Maybe taking walks in parks to connect us with nature. Maybe forging friendships with people who are positive rather than cynical. Maybe praying in ways that invite God to reveal God's love to us.

When we validate people's emotions and then work with them, we bring in the emotional element, which gives depth to the sermon because we touch our listeners' deepest conditions.

- *Story*—People live by stories. That's why Jesus told parables. That's why we watch television and movies, read novels, and tell people about our experiences. Stories are the most powerful ways we communicate. When we tell stories well, they integrate everything else the Heath brothers outline. Stories tend to be simple, unexpected, concrete, credible, and emotional. Some of the best sermons I've ever preached were one or two stories with only a little commentary on the side. Stories and parables were Jesus's favorite way of preaching because he knew they were powerful ways of getting his ideas to stick.

So, I invite you to read *Made to Stick* and see how that may help your preaching. But with that, I also invite you to do more—to look for ways to focus on transformational rather than merely informational preaching and teaching.

NOTES

1. Richard J. Foster, *Celebration of Discipline: The Path to Spiritual Growth* (San Francisco: HarperSanFrancisco, 1998), 1.

2. N. Graham Standish, *Paradoxes for Living: Cultivating Faith in Confusing Times* (Louisville, KY: Westminster John Knox Press, 2001).

3. Thomas R. Kelly, *A Testament of Devotion* (San Francisco: HarperSanFrancisco, 1992).

4. For a free, downloadable resource on formative/spiritual reading and how to create small groups based on spiritual reading, go to http://www.ngrahamstandish.org.

5. Kelly, *A Testament of Devotion*, 40.

6. Continuous positive airway pressure machine.

7. Attention-deficit disorder.

8. For more on Gardner's theories of multiple intelligences, please see Howard Gardner, *Multiple Intelligences: New Horizons in Theory and Practice* (New York: Basic Books, 2006).

9. "Theory of Multiple Intelligences," Wikimedia Foundation, last modified November 4, 2019, 3:35 UTC, https://tinyurl.com/tn36zw7.

10. James Patrick Kinney, "The Cold Within," All Things If, accessed November 19, 2019, https://tinyurl.com/trku2vb.

11. Gillian Tett, *The Silo Effect: The Peril of Expertise and the Promise of Breaking Down Barriers* (New York: Simon & Schuster Paperbacks, 2015), 13.

12. Chip Heath and Dan Heath, *Made to Stick: Why Some Ideas Survive and Others Die* (New York: Random House, 2007).

13. Duke University's Center for the Advancement of Social Entrepreneurship, https://centers.fuqua.duke.edu/case/.

14. SUCCES: Simple Unexpected Concrete Credentialed Emotional Story. Heath and Heath, *Made to Stick*, 18.

15. John F. Kennedy, "Inaugural Address," January 20, 1961, United States Capitol, transcript, https://tinyurl.com/sbjgx93.

16. "You Can't Always Get What You Want," track 4, side 2 on Rolling Stones, *Let It Bleed*, Decca/London, 1969.

8

LEADING THEM FROM HERE TO THERE

Tina is an American Baptist Church pastor of two yoked churches in western Pennsylvania. She has been the pastor of these churches for three years. The churches became yoked prior to her ministry as part of the smaller church's request to be paired with the larger church so it could afford a pastor.

Both churches are in somewhat urban areas, although the smaller of the two is in a more struggling area, and they are about two miles apart. Over time, Tina has become more and more drained by the smaller Mt. Pisgah Baptist Church (Mt. Pisgah), even as she is energized by the larger First Baptist Church (First). First is engaged in mission beyond their church, but Mt. Pisgah resists almost anything outside of the church, other than to give a small sum of money each year to Operation Christmas. Tina finds her situation vexing, proclaiming in a previous session, "How can I be such a good pastor in one church and so dreadful in the other? It makes me feel like Dr. Jekyll and Mr. Hyde!"

We have been meeting for over a year. We initially began our work with a focus on spiritual direction. Over time, we shifted to clergy coaching since it became clear her issues were as much congregational and pragmatic as they were spiritual. We had just begun to talk about the differences between the two churches and her frustrations with Mt. Pisgah in the previous session. She ended that session by saying she felt she had a split personality in leading the two churches.

****

Graham: So, how's life in the realm of split personalities?

Tina: Good question. That's how I feel—Peter with one, Judas with the other.

Graham: Oh my. I hope they don't really see you as Judas.

Tina: Maybe not, but I do feel they sometimes see me as some sinister figure sent to torment them.

Graham: Yikes! What's happened?

Tina: I got frustrated with them and decided they needed a "come to Jesus" moment. So at our last board meeting, I asked them what they wanted for the church. All I got back were blank stares. I kept pushing: "Folks, what's your vision? What's your hope? Where do you see this church in ten or twenty years?" Nothing. I felt like it was a "come to Judas" moment where I was asking, "Would you rather be crucified or stabbed to death?"

Graham: That just sounds frustrating.

Tina: It was!

Graham: And it sounded a bit desperate.

Tina: Desperate? What do you mean?

Graham: Well, you were frustrated with them. You wanted them to do something—live, die, move, stay—just decide something. You've run out of ideas. So you put it on them. You were desperate for them to do or say something, and what you received was a deafening silence. The reason was they didn't know what to say. They remind me of young kids when their parents yell at them, "Why won't you pick up your clothes?" or "Why can't you just do your homework without being asked?"

Tina: Oh, come on! They're not kids. They're adults!

Graham: Are you sure?

Tina: Seriously? Almost all of them are in their fifties, sixties, and seventies.

Graham: Right . . . chronologically. But what about in maturity?

Tina: Again, old!

Graham: Umm . . . okay . . . what about in spiritual maturity?

Tina: I don't know. They've all been in the church for most of their lives. Doesn't that make them mature?

Graham: Nah, just old!

Tina: Nice.

Graham: I think we're good at recognizing people's chronological age, but churches have a spiritual age too. Some churches and their members are very mature—perhaps middle-aged. Some churches are very immature—perhaps just preschoolers. We assume the chronological age matches the spiritual age, but they're not the same thing.

Tina: How do you tell?

Graham: You already know. Let's look at your two churches. If you had to put a spiritual age on both, what would First's spiritual age be compared to Mt. Pisgah's?

Tina: That's a *really* interesting question. What would the difference be? I think First is older. They're not great spiritually, but they're willing to try things. When I ask them to pray, they're much better at it. And when I talk to them about discerning God's will, I think they get it more. I know they're not very mature, but I'd say they're like spiritual tenth-graders. Mt. Pisgah's . . . Oh Gawd! Heh . . . I almost don't want to answer because it sounds insulting.

Graham: It's okay. It helps to be honest about what you feel their age is.

Tina: I think they're like . . . I dunno . . . second-graders?

Graham: What makes them second-graders?

Tina: They're kind of afraid of everything. Man! I never thought about it this way.

Graham: Tell me about their history before you came.

Tina: Well, they've always been a small church. The town they're in was originally a small steel town outside of Pittsburgh. It was a place where immigrants settled. I think our church started because some Welsh workers moved into the area, and I believe the church was built by the people who owned the steel mills. I think it was built so they wouldn't make trouble for the Italians and the Poles who went to the Catholic church.

Graham: How long ago?

185

Tina: Oh, mid- to late-1800s.

Graham: So what do you know about them since then?

Tina: I should, but I don't know much about their early history. I just know they began as a church for the Welsh workers.

Graham: Do you think they ever had a golden age, that period when they were doing really, really well?

Tina: First did. They were different. They were a church built for managers, probably from the same steel mills. They've had several pastors in their history who were very good. They had one in the '20s and '30s, I think. His picture's up on the wall of the library. He was there for a long time, so I guess he did really well. They had another pastor in the '70s and '80s who helped them grow and was a beloved, caring person when the steel mills started closing. He helped them attract members from across the river in Pittsburgh even after many of their members moved away.

Mt. Pisgah? Yeah . . . I don't know if they ever had a golden age. What I do know is over the past thirty years, they've had a string of pastors who never stayed longer than four or five years. Nope, I take that back. They did have one guy who was there for ten years, but I think he suffered from depression and didn't do much. They don't talk about him often, but it sounds like he only preached and attended board meetings. It doesn't even sound as though he visited them in the hospitals much.

Graham: How long ago was he there?

Tina: That's a good question. Maybe twenty years ago. This is interesting. I've not spent much time looking into either church's history.

Graham: What about the pastors since that guy twenty years ago?

Tina: As I said, they all seem to come and go.

Graham: Were they young? Old?

Tina: I think most were older, but a few came there right after seminary.

Graham: And how did they do?

Tina: Well, they're not there anymore, are they?

Graham: No, they're not. You are. So you're saying they weren't very good.

Tina: That's what I thought, but now I'm questioning that. Here I am three years in and I'm thinking about bailing on them. So how good am I?

Graham: Well . . . you are Dr. Jekyll at First.

Tina: I am that!

Graham: If you were to give me a summary of what you *think* the other pastors were like, what would it be?

Tina: I'd think they came in and tried to get them to do something, and then they received blank stares. I know my predecessor probably would say that. I spoke with her several months ago, and she said she reached the point where she was calling out people in her sermons and during meetings. That's how she knew it was time to leave. She was frustrated.

Graham: Where is she now?

Tina: She's a chaplain in a nursing home.

Graham: So, do you think other pastors got frustrated with them and called them out too?

Tina: I wouldn't know, but I'm getting close to being like that.

Graham: Oh my! Don't do that. Actually, do you want to know what your church members sound like to me?

Tina: Sure.

Graham: They sound like neglected dogs. They sound like they're scared to do anything. If they do the right thing, they'll be ignored. If they don't do the right thing, they'll get called out. If they do the absolute wrong thing, they'll be abandoned. Even the pastors who stay neglect them. They remind me of episodes of *The Dog Whisperer*.

Tina: I remember that show.

Graham: Did you ever watch it?

Tina: A bit.

Graham: I was addicted to it. I found it fascinating. I remember several episodes where Cesar Millan, the Dog Whisperer, was dealing with rescue dogs that were scared of everything. Sometimes they were aggressive. Most times, they just cowered and hid under a chair or bed.

He seemed to have a basic approach to help them. At first, he would just sit sideways next to them, although he did hold a tennis racket down near his feet in case he needed protection. He just made sure he didn't hold it in a threatening way. Then he would slowly put his hand near them. The dogs would often sway their heads back and forth, trying to figure out whether to cower or run. He might have given them a treat, I can't remember. Everything he did was gentle but firm at the same time. Eventually, he would put a leash around them and walk them. Taking the dogs for a walk is *big* with the Dog Whisperer. He walked them while holding their leashes taut so they had to walk close to him. Apparently, walking with them and keeping them close made them feel wanted and safe, under the protection of the alpha dog.

After the walk, he'd then pet them and show them affection, but he always kept his energy calm. Everything he did was calm, gentle, but also assertive and directive.

Tina: So my church is a dog? Really?

Graham: Man! You're ornery today!

Tina: I'm tired. I think I'm tired of this church. But I think I'm getting what you're saying. You're saying Mt. Pisgah is like a neglected dog.

Graham: It sounds like that to me. What does it sound like to you?

Tina: Yes. I think so. They may even have been a bit abused culturally. I'm now wondering if, because their church was started by steel companies, the congregation was abused and neglected right from the start. I'd be willing to bet that even though they had their own church, the mill owners and managers constantly put them down. I imagine owners and managers at First criticized and denigrated the members of Mt. Pisgah for years because that's where the workers were. My guess is Mt. Pisgah was always "that" church down there where "those people" went to church.

Wow, I just never thought about it this way. So, when I get angry with them and ask them what they want in a harsh tone, their blank stares aren't just them undermining my ministry. They're like dogs under a bed, scared of everything.

Graham: Are they?

Tina: Yes! So what do you do when your church acts like a bunch of scared dogs?

Graham: I guess you take them for a walk.

Tina: What the hell does that mean?

Graham: It means that my metaphor's breaking down, although it could be that you're called to walk with them as they are, rather than pushing them to be show dogs or assistance dogs or frisbee-catching dogs or obstacle-course dogs.

What we're talking about fits right in with a scale a committee of our presbytery—like your conference—created to help us understand how to help churches. I was asked to chair the Encouraging Churches to Flourish Unit of our presbytery, and our mission was to help our churches grow and to develop programs and training to help our pastors to become better leaders so they could lead healthier churches. We were committed to developing programs and trainings that weren't just the run-of-the-mill ones—that weren't what they would get in seminaries and typical church conferences. We wanted ours to be creative, insightful, and pragmatic.

As part of the process of deciding what to do, we engaged in a three-month study on what's led to the mainline Protestant church's decline and what was significantly helping some churches turn around. As part of that study, we created a scale that's been *hugely* helpful in understanding both where churches are and how to respond. Do you mind if I show you the scale?

Tina: No, go ahead. I'm interested in seeing it, especially if it relates to dogs.

Graham: It does, but only sort of. (laughs) Here's the scale:[1]

Encouraging Churches to Flourish Scale

Tina: Okay, what am I seeing?

Graham: It's a scale representing where churches are spiritually and missionally. We realized churches are all in different places along this scale; but as pastors, we aren't typically aware of that. All of the books, seminars, and workshops about how to create thriving churches have trained us to believe our churches could be similarly thriving *if only* they did *this* or *that*, or one or two things that the authors suggested. These authors—and I may be guilty of this, too—have written as if there were one answer to all of our woes. The problem is most of our churches aren't at the "thriving" end of the scale. Many are at the "surviving" end of the scale, and barely surviving, at that.

Tina: Which brings us to Mt. Pisgah.

Graham: Yeah, Mt. Pisgah. Considering how we've talked about your church, I would say it is at the "surviving" level. You want them to thrive. You want them to be better than they are, but they're barely surviving. And just as yelling at a starving or thirsty dog doesn't help because they don't have the energy to do what you want, neither do our churches. So the congregations stop and give us blank stares. We want them to be a great church, so we urge them to be great. Meanwhile, they're wondering when we'll abandon them like all the others, leaving them to die.

Tina: Whoa! I'm not trying to do that.

Graham: Of course you aren't. The problem isn't what you're trying to do. It's what you have to do to help them be better. Let me take you across the scale and explain what we realized about it. I'm going to describe the different levels. Here's a sheet with descriptions I just printed out, along with another explaining what the challenge is at each level:

- *Surviving*—the level at which churches merely do their best to keep their doors open but have little energy or drive for ministry and mission other than worship and pastoral care.
- *Functioning*—the level at which churches operate as a typical church, having a board and some level of programming, but rarely try anything new or challenging, and are mired in a

190

bygone way of functioning.

- *Experimenting*—the level at which churches function well enough to allow periodic experimentation with something new, whether a new program, a new aspect of worship, or a new mission, yet the experimentation is tentative and rarely lasting.
- *Exploring*—the level at which churches are willing to explore new avenues for worship, ministry, and mission as they sense God calling them; these new avenues often become permanent as churches experience success with them.
- *Serving*—the level at which churches have explored new avenues enough that seeking God's call to service becomes second nature.
- *Thriving*—the level at which churches thrive in every area and ministry becomes relatively easy as they hear God's call constantly and always find God's presence in worship, ministry, and mission.

Tina: They're definitely at survival. Where is First?

Graham: Let me get to that in a second. Here's what we wrote about the task we face at each level. The basic principle is a church can't go from one level to a much higher one in a snap. A church has to work up one level at a time:

- If the church is merely *surviving*, then the "flourishing" task is to get it to *function* better.
- If a church is merely *functioning* as a church typically functions, then the "flourishing" task is to help it begin *experimenting* with new ministries.
- If the church is *experimenting*, then the "flourishing" task is to start *exploring* new ministries and missions regularly.
- If the church is *exploring*, the "flourishing" task is to help it see *serving* others in everything as its vision.
- Finally, if the church is *serving*, the "flourishing" task is to help it *thrive* in every area of congregational life.

Tina: So what's my task with Mt. Pisgah?

Graham: If they're at survival level, then your task is simply to get them functioning better. That means having a somewhat boring-for-you ministry there. The focus is on getting them to do the basic church tasks in a healthier way. So, focus on worship, board meetings, dinners, and other simple functions. You probably won't get them involved in much mission and ministry.

Tina: Roger that!

Graham: You can get them to flirt with ministry two levels up, but not above that. So, your basic task is to get them functioning better while occasionally experimenting with short-term, easy ministries and missions. But that's not where they'll be most of the time. Now, where do you think First is on this scale?

Tina: I've been thinking about that as you talked. I think they are definitely at the "experimenting" level. They function very well. Meetings and worship are really good there. Not any great shakes, but good.

And what you're saying is if they're at the "experimenting" stage, I can push them to explore more. What does that mean?

Graham: It means pushing them to engage in more long-term, adventurous ministries and missions. Do you have any of those?

Tina: We're planning some. We're thinking about creating an afterschool drop-in center where kids come to the church and play games, do homework, watch movies, and have snacks. We have many single- and working-parent families, and our older members wouldn't mind playing with kids.

Graham: So you're already intuitively moving up the scale.

Tina: Yeah! I feel better about what I'm doing. But I always feel better about First. So what does this mean for me at Mt. Pisgah?

Graham: This is where it's difficult. You're the pastor of two very different churches, so you have to be a very different pastor at each, which is a bit unfair. Your preaching at First needs to be more like a cheerleader's, encouraging them to try things. Your preaching at Mt. Pisgah needs to be more like the Dog Whisperer's.

Tina: You mean I have to write two different sermons every Sunday?

Graham: Not necessarily, but you may have to consider two different versions of the same sermon. Let me give you an example of this. Have I told you about how, when I was the pastor of Calvin Presbyterian Church, we were asked to come alongside a struggling church, Trinity Presbyterian Church, to help it grow after a crisis?

Tina: Yeah, that's the one where they had the pastor who caused them to drop from 200 members down to a hundred?

Graham: Um, that would be 200 down to seventeen. By the time we came alongside, they were up to thirty members after a few returned. Reflecting back and using the scale, they were clearly somewhere between surviving and functioning. We didn't come in trying to make them thrive. Instead, we came in where they were and focused on helping them function in a healthy way all across the board. And from there, we started doing experimental mission and ministry. These were small outreach efforts that wouldn't take much time and commitment but that could build confidence. So the first thing we did was Trunk or Treat, which is a—

Tina: Yeah, I know: cars in the parking lot with members in costumes, trunks open with candy inside to give to people.

Graham: It was great for them. They had fourteen families participate, and they felt happy they could do something for the community, even if none of the families who came ever visited the church.

We also experimented with a Sunday brunch program where, before church each Sunday, we'd offer a breakfast of scrambled eggs, bacon, juice, and pastries. For twenty minutes, we'd have an adult study at one table and a kids' study at another. It was relatively low commitment and prep, as well as easy cleanup. It worked for a bit, but it was hard to sustain. The point was this experimenting gave them a sense of confidence.

Tina: Is confidence that important?

Graham: Absolutely, especially for a church at the survival level. When you're at the survival level in anything, you have no confidence. Your perspective shrinks. All you care about is making it through the next hour, day, week, or month. You have no answers and few plans.

Tina: So did the experimenting help?

Graham: Yes, it helped them grow again. We did other things too. We reshaped their worship service to make it simpler and more spiritually accessible to people who may be new to church. During our time with them, they grew from thirty to forty-two members and went from twenty-five to thirty-eight in attendance. When we left, they were much more confident, but they were also functioning in a healthier way.

Tina: What did you do to get them functioning better?

Graham: This is hard to explain, other than to say that in the board meetings we emphasized collaboration on ideas rather than competition, taking time for prayer and study, seeking prayerful consensus—it's all things I wrote about in my book *Becoming a Blessed Church.* There were times when they were at loggerheads, and we would stop the meeting and tell them we didn't care that much about *what* decisions they made, but we did care about *how* they made them. I also emphasized I wouldn't let decisions not made collaboratively pass. They had to decide together. This reduced much of the competitive conflict.

Tina: We're thinking Mt. Pisgah is at survival level?

Graham: It certainly sounds like it.

Tina: So my focus there would simply be on helping them function in a healthier way and experiment with small ministries and missions.

Graham: That would be my suggestion. By the way, Trinity is doing much better now. They have a lay pastor who probably now has them at the "experimenting" level, and he's getting them to explore new ministries and missions together. I think he's doing a great job, and he's a great guy! He has a lot of passion for Christ, for ministry, for them. He has them feeling they can do anything, which I love because I grew to truly like them.

Tina: What does this all mean for me?

Graham: You have two very different churches, which means you have two very different courses of action with them. With First, it sounds like they're somewhere around exploring, so focus on pushing them to become serving, meaning you can help embed a sense of ministry and mission within them so they'll take it on with or without your help. With Mt. Pisgah, you have to be more like the Dog Whisperer and help them come out from under the bed. These are two very different styles of leadership. One requires a more permission-giving approach that encourages them to push the envelope. So with First, you get to be the joyful encourager. The other is like being a trainer where you have to help them feel safe and work with them on developing basic skills. You need to work on trust. With Mt. Pisgah, you have to give them lots of rewards for basic things as you build slowly toward a more engaging ministry.

Tina: Crap! I don't know if I have the energy for that. I like where First is, but I don't know if I have the patience to be a trainer.

Graham: Well, you have choices.

Tina: Like what?

Graham: You can try to treat them both alike, but that's what you're already doing and it's frustrating the heck out of you. You can leave one and stay at the other, or you can leave both and look for another church that fits where you want to be. Just be careful about what you wish for. All pastors are looking for that one church that's at the "thriving" level. I assume about 5 percent of all churches are there. They're rare, and most of them are there because they had a pastor who built them to that level after going through all the others. In the end, I don't think we're called to go to churches at the "thriving" level. I think we're called to build them slowly to that level, whether or not we can actually reach it.

Tina: Ugh! I have some thinking to do.

Graham: And praying. Let me build on what we've been talking about, if that's okay.

Tina: Sure.

Graham: All of this isn't just about building them to the "thriving" level. That's the dream, but I think there's something more important God's calling us to do.

Tina: Which is?

Graham: I think we're called to build communities that embody both the spiritual and the missional.

Tina: Isn't that obvious?

Graham: No, it's not. Think about what we've been discussing. In many ways, we're talking about the kind of ministry you're attracted to and want to do. You want them to thrive. But what if that's not your calling? What if your calling is to build them into a healthier community at whatever level that is?

As pastors we all have ambitions, but the question is whether our ambitions serve our aspirations. This isn't my idea. I learned it from Fr. Adrian van Kaam when I studied for my PhD in formative spirituality. He was the one who started that graduate program. He constantly taught that the spiritual life is one of service to *aspiration* and *inspiration* over *ambition*. The word "ambition" literally means to "strive for favor or applause" and to "go around" in the service of receiving votes or mass approval. When we are ambitious, we strive to be noticed and praised. It's self-focused as we hope others will turn their focus onto us and our achievements. "Aspiration" is a spiritual word because it has the root of the word "spirit": *a spiritus*, or literally moving "toward spirit." To be *inspired* literally means to have "spirit in" us.

I wish I could tell you where van Kaam wrote about this, but I heard it more in lectures and conversations with him. He would say our ambitions can serve our aspirations, but not the other way around. In other words, we can "go around" and seek favor from others in the service of doing what God calls us to do—to do what we feel called to do because we have been prayerfully inspired to do so while pursuing our aspirations, our yearning, to serve God. But aspirations and inspirations can't become secondary to ambitions, because ambitions will wipe out aspirations. When our focus is on our receiving attention and applause, we'll end up serving ourselves rather than God because we put ourselves, our will, and our desires over what God wants. So, ambitions can serve aspirations, but aspirations can't serve ambitions.

Tina: Okay, so what you're saying is if my ambition to get both of my churches thriving drives everything else, then it will start becoming too much about me and not enough about serving God in leading them as these churches are. Does that make sense?

Graham: Yes.

Tina: And so I have to focus on getting them to where God wants them to be, not to where I want them to be.

Graham: Yes, although the struggle between ambition and aspiration is very hard because we all want to be seen as successful. In fact, our future careers depend upon it.

Tina: Crap! Which means I may never be successful at Mt. Pisgah.

Graham: Maybe not successful the way ambition measures it; but if you build a healthier community where they can become less fearful and more faithful, that would be an amazing thing. Remember, you told me you're not sure if they ever had confidence in themselves. They've never felt successful. They've always felt like a neglected dog.

Tina: You said that, not me.

Graham: Whatever, yeah, I guess I did. Anyway, the point is that success for them may be building a more confident community, even if they'll never become this big, noticed church.

Tina: And I keep wanting to turn them into that big, noticed church.

Graham: We all do. That's our ambition urging us to be noticed, to be applauded, to be praised. But that's not what God calls us to do.

Tina: How do I build that community?

Graham: You mean give you the secret to it all in the last ten minutes of our session?

Tina: Sure! Is that too much to ask—to give me all the knowledge I want in the space of ten minutes?

Graham: If I only had a chip I could stick into your head.

Tina: That would be nice.

Graham: Okay, let me take a stab at it. Since most people like to think in threes, let me see if I can come up with three ways to build this kind of community. First I would say *the overriding rule has to be that relationships matter above all else.*

Tina: Right, relationships matter.

Graham: Above all else. I'm not saying above devotion to God, but I am saying we're called to lead communities—literally "unities with others"—that prize collaboration, consensus, compassion, companionship, cooperation, communion, and all those other "with" words.

Tina: "*With*" words?

Graham: Yeah. In that list I just gave you, all the words have pre-fixes that mean "with"—co, con, com. How does this translate into how you lead them? It means thinking of meetings as places to forge healthy relationships rather than places simply to make decisions. We hate committees (another "with" word) because we hate the process of having to deal with people's personalities when making decisions since it would be easier to make them by ourselves.

Tina: Roger that.

Graham: But there's a way of approaching committees where we realize the decisions are secondary. Remember when I told you about the session at Trinity? How I told them I cared more about *how* they made decisions rather than *what* decisions they made?

Tina: Yeah.

Graham: That's the difference. Over time, I actually began to see meetings as a primary place to forge relationships. At Calvin Church, we set up our meetings so they all started with fifteen to thirty minutes of prayer and study where people could discuss spiritual quotes about how to discern or discover God. And instead of always driving them to stay on agenda and "decide things," we allowed for chitchat and digressions because that is how people form relationships. The connections bonded them, not the decisions. Or better yet, how decisions were made bonded them. Meetings became an important time, and doing this turned committee meetings into small groups.

Tina: Okay, this is different. I have to think more about this. Turn all meetings into relationship-building times.

Graham: Yes, because it's all about relationships. A second thought is for you to *focus your preaching on ideas that build community.* Our culture tends to have our sermons address the individual struggles we have, or address abstract ideas about God and life. That's not wrong, but building communities through sermons means focusing much more on how to forge healthier relationships. Looking back, I realize I focused on how to form healthier relationships with God and with others in many of my sermons. That can lead into ministry and mission sermons, but the focus still needs to be more on community-building.

Tina: Can you give me an example?

Graham: Yeah . . . um . . . here's one. I have a stump sermon I use for when I talk about Samaritan and what we do—our counseling, spiritual direction, coaching, and consulting. I talk about the nature of the Good Samaritan versus that of the priest and the Levite. I talk about how the priest and the Levite were so focused on themselves, their purity, and their ability to fulfill their obligations that they saw helping the injured man as an impediment to their jobs. The Samaritan, who would have been despised and rejected by the priest and Levite for being part of a false religion, was the one who saw the injured man as a neighbor, as someone to whom he was connected. And that connection, that desire for relationship with a stranger, led him to tend to him, try to heal him, and come back and care for him.

I then talk about how we're called to connect with, and care for, those whom everyone else ignores because it's inconvenient to care. Even more, I talk about how to be a Samaritan—we're called to care for people even if it means we may be rejected, hurt, falsely accused. The Samaritan certainly could have been accused of covering his tracks by caring for the man he had beaten.

Then I might have given them three steps to become Samaritans: (1) Never be too busy to care for the people around us. (2) Always look for those who need help, whether close to us or strangers. (3) Let God guide us along the way so we can become people of love.

Tina: Okay.

Graham: Let's see if there's a third . . . Got it! *Be a leader obsessed with relationships rather than success.* In other words, don't see yourself as the pastor who's in charge of fixing the church and all these people so you can be considered a success. Think of it as God has put you in a place where you can love them and be loved in return. Don't focus on how well they love you. Focus on how well you love them. They'll hurt you at times, criticize you, doubt you, correct you. Be gracious in return and model healthy relationships. Be the leader who causes them to want to become better people by example.

The nicest compliment I ever received from anyone was from a member of Calvin Church who said to me, a little before I left the church to come to Samaritan, that the thing that made the most difference to her was she wanted to become a better person when she was around me. Not because she wanted to please me or receive my approval, but because she felt I treated her better than others did and she wanted to be like that. I'm getting teary thinking about that because she had a big influence on my life.

Tina: I see that. So, let me see if I can remember the three. First, it's all about relationships. Second . . . um . . .

Graham: Yeah, what was that?

Tina: Oh yeah, teach them how to form healthier relationships. Third, focus on relationships over success.

Graham: That's it! And with the final one, I think that's what God wants most. Have you ever read *The Great Divorce* by C. S. Lewis?

Tina: I don't know. What's it about?

Graham: It's about a guy who dies and goes to Hell, but Hell isn't a place of fire and punishment. It's just a dreary English city or town where people do mundane things all day long. They play bridge, eat roasts, and endure constant rain and drizzle.

Every Thursday, though, they can take a bus trip to the outskirts of Heaven. It's like stopping just outside the gates of Yellowstone. You can see beautiful mountains, streams, lakes, and forests inside Heaven. People come out from Heaven and beg the people on the bus to join them by simply choosing to be with God. Unfortunately, these bus trippers make excuses for why they can't—they have a roast in the oven, they have to visit a friend, things like that. They're like the priest and Levite. They think they have better things to do.

Anyway, there's one scene in the book that I love. The narrator, who is visiting Heaven, is given a Scottish guide. At one point they see a parade of people and animals weaving in and out of Heaven. They're celebrating a woman as they sing and dance. Let me read it to you because I won't do it justice by describing it. (reaches for the book and thumbs through the pages) Here it is. Listen to what Lewis says:

"Is it? . . . is it?" I whispered to my guide.

"Not at all," said he. "It's someone ye'll never have heard of. Her name on Earth was Sarah Smith and she lived at Golders Green."

"She seems to be . . . well, a person of particular importance?"

"Aye. She is one of the great ones. Ye have heard that fame in this country and fame on Earth are quite different things."

[. . .]

"And who are all these young men and women on each side?"

"They are her sons and daughters."

"She must have had a very large family, Sir."

"Every young man or boy that met her became her son—even if it was only the boy that brought the meat to her back door. Every girl that met her was her daughter."

[. . .]

"Every beast and bird that came near her had its place in her love. In her they became themselves. And now the abundance of life she has in Christ from the Father flows into them."[2]

Tina: In other words, God measures our success by relationships, not by size or programs or ministry or mission.

Graham: Yes, and that's enough for today.

Tina: I'm going to be thinking about this. I'm not sure *what* to think about all of this, but I'll think about all of this.

Graham: Great!

FURTHER THOUGHTS

The process of creating the Encouraging Churches to Flourish Scale was a tremendous experience because it helped all of us better understand what the challenges are in trying to help a church become healthier and, we hope, grow. I'm certain anyone could take that scale and add a hundred other little stages along the way, and perhaps they would be more insightful. Still, the scale clarified that the mainline Protestant church's task isn't just to grow from some neutral platform. We're growing from a deficit.

All of the mainline Protestant denominations are in decline. I don't even have to cite a source for this, because if you Google "mainline Protestant church decline," the pages go on and on and on. I can't find research on what the ratio is of churches in decline versus growing ones, but I would be willing to bet it's an 80/20 ratio of decline to growth, and that may be low. I know when I was the pastor of my church, we were one of the few churches in our presbytery that grew consistently in membership every year.

What the scale really helped with is understanding the task we face as pastors if we're to turn around churches. Too often we come into a church as pastors and assume we're starting with a relatively neutral foundation upon which to build. But we're not. We assume we're building a church on something like a grassy field we just have to dig up a bit, lay some foundation stone, and then build up. In reality, many of us go into churches that are like brownfields. I don't know if you know what a brownfield is. They are a reality of living in western Pennsylvania.

Back in the 1970s and early 1980s, most of the steel mills that had been here for generations were closed down as competition from Europe and Japan destroyed the local steel economy. Today, there are very few steel mills remaining in western Pennsylvania. What we have left are brownfields, the dirt field that remained when the steel plants were torn down and all the scrap was hauled away. Most, if not all, of those leftover fields are toxic. Fifty to a hundred years of steelmaking allowed toxic metals, ash, and chemicals to leach into the ground.

Some of these old steel mills have been turned into outdoor malls and upscale condos and houses; but before that could happen, much work had to be done to ensure the buildings were safe places to work and live. In many cases, federal superfunds had to be used to dig deep down and remove the toxic, and sometimes radioactive, soil. The reclamation work took many years to finally remove the toxic soil and lay a foundation that was safe and adequate for building. Interestingly, the Pittsburgh Steelers and the University of Pittsburgh's football team share a practice facility built atop a brownfield.

In many ways, our churches have become like brownfields.

Decades of decline have created toxicity in churches as ongoing conflict, communal depression, or learned helplessness has afflicted them. The work of a pastor in these churches may be to spend years cleaning things up and preparing the place for growth. If the church is mired in conflict, the pastor may have to spiritually and emotionally don a hazmat suit that protects them from the toxicity. That means building a personal community of support outside of the church, as well as the steely courage inside the church, to do the work of cleaning out the toxicity. If the church is mired in helplessness, the pastor may have to find ways to encourage members to take care of the church to prepare it for the possibility of growth.

The issue for many pastors is often we're ignorant of where the church is, so we begin our leadership by offering a vision and approach that simply won't work in their situation. For example, constantly pushing a church in survival mode to do more mission will frustrate them and us. The issue isn't that they won't look beyond themselves—they *can't* look beyond themselves. They're in survival mode; and just as a cornered or threatened animal will bite, so will members of a church in survival mode that's pushed too hard to do what they're scared to do. Our task as leaders is to attend to their survival needs. We have to help them feel safe, we have to feed them where they are, and we have to nurture them to greater health.

Another way of thinking about all of this is to consider Abraham Maslow's hierarchy of needs.[3] Maslow was a psychology professor at Brandeis University in the mid-twentieth century. He developed a groundbreaking theory that all humans have a hierarchy of needs that must be met for us to thrive. According to his theory, we cannot attend to higher-level needs unless we first satisfy and secure more foundational needs.

According to Maslow, the most foundational needs are *physiological* needs—for food, water, air, warmth, sleep. If we don't have these, nothing else matters. When we're lacking these, we can't focus on anything else. Beyond those are *security* needs—for shelter and safety. Beyond those are *love/belonging* needs—for connection, interaction, and intimacy. Beyond those are *esteem* needs, which are the needs to feel confident and a sense of worth that comes from accomplishment. Finally, at the pinnacle, are *self-actualization* needs, which are the hardest to define. Self-actualization means being truly creative, achieving our full potential, and having a sense of purpose and meaning.

Adrian van Kaam, whom I mentioned before and with whom I studied for my PhD, was a friend of Maslow. In fact, van Kaam taught Maslow's classes at Brandeis several times when Maslow went on sabbatical. He argued to us (and apparently with Maslow) that our needs extend beyond those articulated by Maslow. He argued that while self-actualization is important, there are also *transcendent* needs beyond self-actualization. These are the needs to respond to the world with compassion and love, as well as to transcend, which can mean reaching beyond typical human limits (i.e., to explore the unknown and grow beyond our limits) and to connect with the divine (spiritual needs).

Maslow's hierarchy and van Kaam's added level speak to our ministry to churches. Wherever our churches are, our task is to satisfy whatever their most crucial needs are and to help them grow into the next level. Maslow was adamant that to grow into a particular level of human needs, we first have to satisfy the one below it. The same is true with the church. If a congregation is struggling with its survival, then we have to help it feel safe. If the members feel safe, then we can push them to nurture a more caring relationship within the community. If they have nurtured those relationships with each other, then we can help them gain a sense of esteem and confidence in who they are. If they've become confident, we can nurture them to develop a sense of meaning and purpose in everything they do. And if they have that sense of meaning and purpose, they can become increasingly selfless and other-focused in ministry and mission. I'm not saying ministry and mission aren't possible at the lower levels. They are, but congregations won't necessarily become "missional"—committed to a life mission—if they lack security. If they feel the church could close soon, or they can't afford a pastor, or there is persistent, ongoing conflict, they can't focus on mission.

This insight about the need to feel safe isn't just according to the scale we offered earlier or Maslow's hierarchy of needs. You find it reflected in Scripture. Jesus nurtured his disciples—feeding them, helping them feel safe and loved, and giving them a sense of purpose—before sending them out in mission:

> These twelve Jesus sent out with the following instructions: "Go nowhere among the Gentiles, and enter no town of the Samaritans, but go rather to the lost sheep of the house of Israel. As you go, proclaim the good news, 'The kingdom of heaven has come near.' Cure the sick, raise the dead, cleanse the lepers, cast out demons. You received without payment; give without payment. Take no gold, or silver, or copper in your belts, no bag for your journey, or two tunics, or sandals, or a staff; for laborers deserve their food. Whatever town or village you enter, find out who in it is worthy, and stay there until you leave. As you enter the house, greet it. If the house is worthy, let your peace come upon it; but if it is not worthy, let your peace return to you. If anyone will not welcome you or listen to your words, shake off the dust from your feet as you leave that house or town. Truly I tell you, it will be more tolerable for the land of Sodom and Gomorrah on the day of judgment than for that town."[4]

Reflecting on the scripture, we see that Jesus didn't just send them out after inviting his disciples to follow him. They were trained over two or more years. It was only when they were ready that they were sent out in mission. Similarly, we have to nurture and train our members in ways that help them gain confidence before we expect them to be deeply engaged in mission.

I invite you, using the exercise below, to reflect on where your congregation may be and what leadership approach may be necessary to help your congregation become healthier and grow.

LEADERSHIP FOCUS EXERCISE

1. Read the scale levels described below and reflect on where your church may be on it.

- *Surviving*—the level at which churches merely do their best to keep their doors open but have little energy or drive for ministry and mission other than worship and pastoral care.
- *Functioning*—the level at which churches operate as a typical church, having a board and some level of programming, but rarely try anything new or challenging, and are mired in a bygone way of functioning.
- *Experimenting*—the level at which churches function well enough to allow periodic experimentation with something new, whether a new program, a new aspect of worship, or a new mission, yet the experimentation is tentative and rarely lasting.
- *Exploring*—the level at which churches are willing to explore new avenues for worship, ministry, and mission as they sense God calling them; these new avenues often become permanent as churches experience success with them.
- *Serving*—the level at which churches have explored new avenues enough that seeking God's call to service becomes second nature.
- *Thriving*—the level at which churches thrive in every area and ministry becomes relatively easy as they hear God's call constantly and always find God's presence in worship, ministry, and mission.

2. Respond to the following: "My church seems to be at the _____ level because of the following attributes I've noticed." Focus on the overall church, not particular elements, since a church may be at a lower level in general but have higher-level functioning in specific areas.
3. Based on your description above, reflect on how to adjust your leadership to the level where the church currently is. Write down pragmatic and concrete ways you can address the issues of that level.
4. Based on what you've written above, in what concrete and pragmatic ways can you help the congregation begin to move to the next level?

NOTES

1. This scale was created in April 2017 as part of the work of Beaver-Butler Presbytery's Encouraging Churches to Flourish Unit. Members of the unit were the Rev. Dena Roy, the Rev. Jordan Rimmer, Elder Allen Kitchen, the Rev. Dr. N. Graham Standish, the Rev. Derek Marotta, and Elder Ruthie Pickett, with adjunct members the Rev. Connie Frierson and the Rev. Mark Boyd.

2. C. S. Lewis, *The Great Divorce: A Dream* (New York: HarperOne, 1946), 118–20.

3. Many websites and resources explain Maslow's hierarchy of needs. For perhaps the simplest explanation, go to the Simple Psychology website at https://www.simplypsychology.org/maslow.html.

4. Matthew 10:5–15.